A Message to Readers

Congratulations.

Buying *The Student's Memory Book* may be the best academic decision you've ever made, because you are on your way to developing a virtually unlimited memory. As you peruse these chapters, you will quickly acquire the power to remember everything you read or hear. There will be almost nothing that you can't learn.

The Student's Memory Book is structured around courses you'll be taking in mathematics, chemistry, geology, foreign language, economics, geography, history, physics, biology, and political science. So besides giving you an immeasurable memory, *The Student's Memory Book* will give you a head start—and a major edge—in those courses.

The Student's
Memory Book

The Student's Memory Book

BILL ADLER, JR.

Doubleday
New York London Toronto Sydney Auckland

Published by Doubleday, a division of Bantam Doubleday Dell Publishing Group, Inc., 666 Fifth Avenue, New York, New York 10103.

Doubleday and the portrayal of an anchor with a dolphin are trademarks of Doubleday, a division of Bantam Doubleday Dell Publishing Group, Inc.

Library of Congress Cataloging-in-Publication Data
Adler, Bill, 1956-
The student's memory book / Bill Adler, Jr. --1st ed.
   p.   cm.
1. Mnemonics. 2. Study, Method of. 3. College student
   orientation. I. Title.
   BF385.A34 1988
   153.1'4--dc19   88-9581

ISBN 0-385-24559-9

To my grandmother, who showed me what good memories are about.

Acknowledgments

My dear friend Carol Dana once again has helped turn an ill-coordinated bunch of notions and sentences into a book. She was always available when I called to ask, "Carol, can I read you this paragraph?" I want to thank Carol, the best editor in the nation's capital, for taking the time to read the manuscript and make it good.

Without Jane Dystel, my agent, *The Student's Memory Book* might never have come to be. She encouraged and cajoled and turned an idea into a book.

Harold Levin and Debra Leopold, who run Washington's First Class school, were the original source for this book. When I first approached them in 1984 about teaching my memory techniques to Washington's students, lawyers, consultants, and government workers, they fortunately said yes.

When Doubleday picks executive editors, they pick the best. Leslie Pockell's ideas and changes were 99 percent on the mark (the other 1 percent has to do with my obstinacy), and I am amazed at how smart he is.

I thought there was no better editor. However, when Rachel Klayman took over my book after Les left Doubleday, I was even more amazed. I am indebted to Rachel and pleased she became my editor.

Marian Menzel's fine illustrations helped make this a book pleasing to the eye.

A book's never done till it's done. Peggy Robin's thorough examination of the galleys and her suggestions provided the final polish to *The Student's Memory Book.*

Contents

Introduction

There's a subject that practically no school or university teaches, even though the information in that course is essential to learning every other subject: **Memory.**

When you think about it, it makes absolute sense that memory should be a prerequisite to every course. There isn't a single subject that doesn't involve considerable memorization. Every exam tests memorization. Classroom participation is an exercise in revealing your memory—or lack of it. Weekends are spent memorizing. Sweat, anxiety, moderate hysteria, worry, coffee, fast, fatty foods, formulas, definition, equations, names and dates—all these get mixed together when involved with memorization. Physics, math, Chaucer, history, economics, geography—every single subject requires dozens of hours of memorization a semester. And when you combine all those subjects, that's a lot of hours spent doing one thing: **memorizing.**

What's ironic about memory not being a prerequisite is that many subjects such as physics, organic chemistry, short story writing, and international affairs require prerequisites. Teachers insist that you have certain knowledge and skills before you take their courses. The same should be true for memory. *Knowing how to remember is fundamental to everything else in school.*

But how to remember isn't taught. *The Student's Memory Book* will fill that dangerous academic gap.

The material and examples in *The Student's Memory Book* closely follow the curriculum used in most college and advanced high school courses. So in addition to acquiring powerful memory skills, you will be learning specific knowledge you need to know for calculus, economics (especially if you use Samuelson's *Economics),* organic chemistry (especially if you use Morrison and Boyd or Cramm and Hammond), first-year physics, political science, various histories (art history, American history, and the history of science), and other subjects.

The absence of memory instruction in school is absurd. After all, the techniques are easily learned and incredibly powerful. People with trained memories (and you will soon be one) never have to worry about forgetting information, because they don't. Once you've acquired memory skills you can learn anything swiftly and permanently. To trained memorizers, remembering is the opposite of a chore—it's as effortless and as fun as curling up in bed with a paperback novel.

Why Mnemonics Isn't Taught

There are a handful of reasons—none of them sensible—why mnemonics isn't taught in school. Reason number one:

If every student had the kind of memory you will soon possess, courses would have to be structured differently. Exams that evaluate information retention (most tests) would have to be discarded, because learning facts would become the easiest part of any course. As a result, instructors would have to emphasize the less testable aspects of education: reasoning ability, writing skills, ability to draw inferences, and the ability to create new knowledge out of the old. These are more difficult notions to teach—and especially to test. If everyone had a superior memory, drastic changes would be required in teaching and textbooks.

The second reason mnemonics is ignored as a subject is that teachers don't know mnemonics. There's a circular problem: If teachers aren't taught mnemonics, then they can't teach it to their students. Most instructors know more about how their toaster works than how their students remember and forget. Mnemonics is a subject unto itself, and has to be studied just like auto mechanics, linguistics, fractal mathematics, or Chaucer.

Third, although mnemonics is thousands of years old, and despite the fact that memory systems work—far, far better than rote memorization—mnemonics hasn't been rigorously developed as an academic subject. People don't earn degrees in it, and there are no titles such as Associate Memorizer. Professors shy away from teaching subjects that don't fall into already existing academic categories. But despite the lack of academic standing, memory techniques are as useful as knowing how to type, do math, or understand a Shakespeare sonnet.

Not surprisingly, most professional memorizers come from outside academics. Most mnemonists encounter these skills by accident or out of curiosity. I first heard about mnemonics when I saw a paperback about the subject in a used book sale. It sounded interesting and I had time to read the whole book, as I had it along with me while waiting in line to have my driver's license renewed. I read the book, read some more, and practiced what I learned. My only regret is that I didn't learn mnemonics while in school.

The fourth reason memory systems are as rare on campus as free textbooks is that many people regard mnemonics as a gimmick. Because mnemonics isn't part of the mainstream of education, it is ignored. Educators think that memory techniques aren't real learning. In part that's true, because the mere accumulation of facts and figures doesn't make you smart if you don't know how to apply that information. But mnemonics is analogous to calculators and word processors —it is a powerful tool. No one would insist that students return to using slide rules or abandon word processors in favor of mere electronic typewriters. Calculators, word processors (along with their spelling checkers and built-in thesauruses) are accepted because they enable students to spend less time on the mechanical, repetitious, noneducational aspects of learning, and to focus instead on thinking. This is exactly what mnemonics does. By eliminating the tedious aspect of learning—memorization—mnemonics enables students to focus on analyzing, creating, and exploring new ideas.

Fifth, memorization (repetition repetition repetition repetition repetition repetition) is *supposed* to be hard work. The harder you work and the more you suffer, the better you will be, some teachers think. Something that's effortless and effective—like mnemonics—is not supposed to be part of the school curriculum, and isn't. Rote memorization involves brute cerebral force, and therefore some teachers are more comfortable with it.

Finally, mnemonics runs counter to the way most school curriculums are organized. Information is taught one step at a time, with what is currently being taught based on previous material. Information is usually isolated and presented in a logical fashion. (Unfortunately, the world isn't organized linearly: events affect other events in all directions.) Analogies to other events are rare, even when they are relevant: The normal focus on material is narrow and serialist, concentrating on one problem at a time. On the other hand, mnemonics requires a holistic approach to processing information: you must look for connections between various topics and you have to make analogies. With mnemonics you have to see how one piece of information can relate to something else. Logical thinking is the mainstream of what's taught in school; mnemonics requires less structured, even idiosyncratic, thinking.

If integrated into school curriculum, mnemonics would transform every ordinary student into an information warehouse. We may still be decades away from its becoming a part of what's commonly taught, but *you* are only hours away from acquiring a reliable and limitless memory. And once you eliminate memorization as a time-consuming, painful task, you can focus on the more important aspects of learning —using what you know to create new ideas. (And you will have more time to have fun.)

About Memory

Few people brag about their foibles—except when it comes to memory. In the retention department, just about everyone admits to having a poor memory. Perhaps you want an excuse for when you forget names and birthdays; perhaps it's a rationalization that lets you cope with less than perfect exam scores. But whatever the reason you *think* you have a bad memory, you do not have a poor memory.

What you and most other people have is an untrained memory. You simply haven't learned the skills you need to retain information in a simple, confident way. Memory has to be taught. The memory techniques in *The Student's Memory Book* are based on scientific studies of how the brain remembers and, perhaps more important, what works.

You can never assume that you'll remember something. You have to *do* something to ensure that you remember. *The*

Student's Memory Book shows you how simple these things you have to do are.

How to Use This Book

It's worthwhile reading every chapter even if you aren't taking the subject that chapter teaches. The chapters are designed to fulfill two functions: first, to help you learn and practice memory techniques, and second, to serve as an introduction to various substantive subjects, so that you can converse about them, or possibly even take an exam in them. The more you practice these memory techniques—especially in subjects you know little about—the better you will become.

Oh yes. One more thing. As you read this book, you'll quickly discover that using *The Student's Memory Book* is fun, too.

Keep in Mind

Developing an unlimited memory is among the most effortless skills you'll ever learn. Memory skills flow lucidly from the pages on this book to your brain because they work the way your mind likes to work. The brain likes patterns, interesting images, clever sounds, and having fun—and that's the basic stuff of mnemonics. In contrast, the brain loathes boredom and repetition—and that's the way rote memorization, the way you've been remembering all along, works.

Mnemonics is based on four principles. When you want to remember something:

1. *You must want to learn the information.*
2. *You must decide what you want to remember.*
3. *You must focus on the information.*
4. *You must organize the information into memorable categories.*

These four rules are a process: First you want to learn something; then you decide what to learn and what's not important; then you concentrate on it; then organize it into categories using mnemonics.

The first three principles are obvious, though they are frequently ignored by most teachers and students.

The fourth principle, organizing the information and turning it into mnemonics, is what the rest of the *The Student's Memory Book* is about.

About the Examples

As you read this book, keep in mind that the skills you learn are much more important than the information about particular subjects. Although the exercises are designed to be fun and reflect the information you'll have to learn in your courses, it is the mnemonic techniques that are the main ingredients of *The Student's Memory Book.*

Imagery

Imagery, as you will find out in a couple of pages, is a vital part of memory (although not the only technique). Visualization, a vastly underrated skill in general, is almost totally ignored by people who practice rote memorization. Because most people let their mind's eye atrophy, using mental pictures may seem a little awkward, and even a bit difficult initially (though fortunately it is fun). Don't worry about that; you will get better as you practice.

And now, when you turn the page, you will be on your way to acquiring a memory that will catapult you into the fascinating—and valuable—mental world of mnemonics.

PART ONE

Acquiring an Unlimited Memory

1

The First Memory Principles

This chapter takes about an hour to read and digest. No strange theories or complicated processes are discussed in it (or anywhere else in the book). By the end of this chapter you will have learned the principles behind a limitless memory, and *you will have acquired most of the skills you need to remember everything.* You will be on your way to becoming part of an elite group who can digest quantities of information that would overwhelm most mortal students and teachers!

Surprise Seeing, the First Skill

The main ingredient to a first-rate memory is **surprise seeing**.* Surprise seeing is the process of seeing something that strikes a visual, creative, and memorable chord in your brain. Surprise seeing is a visual skill. It is the nexus of a perfect memory because: *We most easily remember facts that strike fancy in our mind's eye.*

Think about the most embarrassing moment of your life, the scariest moment, or the happiest occasion. These events come to mind quickly; in fact, once you think of them, the event may begin to re-create itself in your mind, like a movie. The images—and likely the feelings, too—are clear.

You remember best those things you like or like to do. Persons or processes that have personal meaning for you are easily and permanently implanted in your memory. When you're attracted to somebody of the opposite sex, you have no trouble easily incorporating details—what she's wearing, how his face looks—about that person into your brain. It's easy to remember an event that you njoyed, even if that event took place decades ago.

Surprise seeing helps you convert mundane information, like physics formulas or plot summaries of Shakespeare's plays, into images that you enjoy remembering.

The key to remembering is to turn ordinary, lifeless notions into bold, brilliant, spectacular images. How do you stop a shark from attacking? If you don't know the answer, once I mention how you accomplish that feat you'll never forget: Punch the shark in the nose. See the action as it might happen. Now you'll never forget because punching a shark in the nose is a strange-looking thing to do. How do you stop a lion from charging? (No, you don't take away its credit card.) Spit in its face. Can you picture yourself doing that? Once

---

* I am indebted to Katharine McKenna, who invented this term to describe the geometric toys she created. McKenna's toys, which are visually striking, all involve learning through doing and seeing things in new and surprising ways.

you have the image in your head, you'll never forget about sharks and lions.

Surprise seeing is, in short, turning ordinary information and concepts into images. It is *seeing* what ordinarily would just be expressed verbally.

The better your image of something, the easier it is to remember, and the longer you'll retain that information.

As a student, you might see hundreds of people during the course of a day. Most you don't remember, and you have no reason to remember who they are. Our senses are overwhelmed by information; if everything we saw, heard, tasted, felt, or smelled registered in a significant way in our brains, we'd probably go crazy. Perhaps by anatomical design, perhaps by training, our minds focus on those details that are unique. But out of the hundreds of people your eye comes across, a few—maybe somebody sporting blue hair, or wearing a raincoat on a sunny August day—you do remember. These people stick in your mind because they stand out from the crowd. These people create clear, strong images in your mind and force your mind to pay attention to them. These people are unusual not because of what they look like, but because of the kind of images and mental patterns they create in your head. These unusual images stick to our brain cells like peanut butter; everything else washes away like soap.

Surprise seeing converts the dull and ordinary into the interesting and spectacular. It turns physics formulas or economics definitions into something your brain enjoys learning.

Surprise seeing works like this: Say you want to remember your umbrella. Ever forget an umbrella? Umbrellas are pretty hard to remember, unless you do something visual with them. Imagine your mother hitting you over the head with an umbrella because you lost yours. Don't just think the words: see the scene as vividly as you can. Run that scene over in your mind until you can almost feel the pain. Now you'll remember the umbrella.

The Link, the Second Skill

The second element to a perfect memory is the **link**, or **image association**. The link is simply a visual filing system, a management tool. What the link does is create a frame of reference, a storage point, so that when you want to recall something, you know where it is. You're familiar, I'm sure, with the saying "It's on the tip of my tongue." You may have even uttered those words while you frantically racked your brain for the answer to some question. When the tip-of-the-tongue feeling happens, you haven't actually forgotten the information. The information is there, but your brain just doesn't know where, among the billion and billions of other data it has stored, to look. The link makes the connection between what you want to remember and the memory.

A link is simply a connection between things you want to remember. The linking association between these objects should be as detailed and vivid as you can make it. Say you want to remember your umbrella *and* your hat. Imagine your mother hitting you with the umbrella. Your head is getting pretty sore. Put the hat on to protect your head. See the hat as you would in a photograph. Instead of going **whack**, the umbrella only goes **thud** as it hits the hat. You've linked umbrella and hat so that the two objects are fused into one image. And because you've used surprise seeing, the whole scene is part of your permanent memory.

When the time comes—when you are about to leave the house umbrellaless—your mind will spark to life with the image you've created. The problem of remembering the umbrella won't be a problem at all because of the imprint this image has made. (Why this is so will be discussed later in the book.)

These images, and the techniques that follow, are called mnemonics. Mnemonics is the term used to describe memory systems in general, and specific techniques in particular.

Enough theory for the moment. Let's put this into practice

right away, so you can have a taste for what it's like to possess an unlimited memory. What follows is a list of unrelated objects. Read the list and try to memorize it by rote. Go over it a few times. Then put the list aside for five minutes. Make a phone call, listen to some music, eat—do something other than work on the list. After five minutes see how many of these fifteen items you can recall in the order they are written.

The List

Suitcase
Vitamin tablet
Scotch whisky
Staple
Empire State Building
Punch (the verb)
Diamond
Butter
Rose
Light bulb
Business card
Typewriter
Toothpaste
Shoes
Frog

If you have an above average memory you probably got about 60 percent—that's the equivalent of a D, depending on how the exam is graded. More than likely, the items you managed to memorize weren't even in the right order. (Lucky for you the grading is on a curve.)

But when you put these two memory systems, surprise seeing and the link, together, remembering the list is effortless—and permanent.

Visualize (that's surprise seeing) a **suitcase** in a strange way —in some fashion that does not exist in nature. You might see a **suitcase** sleeping in your bed (with a head, arms, and legs of sorts) or you might picture a **suitcase** popping out of a toaster. Alternatively, imagine a giant suitcase in the middle of the room in which you are standing. Don't limit your image to convention—let your imagination reach its outer reaches. Remember, this is *surprise seeing.* The next step is to create a *link* between **suitcase** and **vitamin** tablet. Associate these images in whatever way your mind is attracted to. You could anthropomorphize again and see a human-like vitamin carrying a suitcase. Do you see the "Vitamin B_{12}" or "Vitamin C" across the vitamin's chest? Or just as easily, you might watch thousands and thousands of vitamins falling out of a suitcase that's suspended in air. Select the image that seems most natural to your mind, and select whatever first leaps at you. Give the image detail, vitality: introduce action, vivid color, out-of-proportion size, sensuality or sex (nobody can peek into your mind and see what's going on; if you're smiling because of the picture, people will probably just think you got a date for Saturday). And keep this in mind: the *words* "suitcase" and "vitamin" are irrelevant—it's the images that are important.

You are developing the ability to remember visually, which is different from the traditional, verbal method you're used to remembering with.

Once you've secured a good picture and can see it, move on to the next item. You only need to work on one set of items at a time. It's much simpler and more effective to focus on two objects at a time, so really don't even let the previous items enter into your consciousness. Because each object on the list is linked, you will remember the previous information when the times comes.

Forget about the suitcase and just link **vitamin** to **scotch whisky**. Perhaps you see the thousands of vitamins falling into the scotch bottle. (There are alternative images: a two-story bottle of scotch whisky balancing on a vitamin. Or your imagination might go in a different direction: as you watch an

X-ray movie of a friend swallowing a vitamin, the vitamin turns into a bottle of scotch whisky. You can use these, but it's better to retain the same image of the vitamin from the previous scene.)

Anthropomorphizing, visualizing multitudes of whatever it is that you are trying to remember, or making an object into a giant version of itself are three good forms of surprise seeing. But you must *see* the image: Only your mind's eye is connected directly to your memory.

Make the same kind of image association with **scotch whisky** and **staple**. Have you ever imagined what a scotch whisky bottle would look like with lots of staples in it? Or maybe the bottle pours staples instead of liquid.

Although I'm creating the pictures for you, it's much better if you produce your own images. Creating your own pictures will make the list (or whatever you're learning) even more memorable. Not only will your own images be more vivid than mine, but *the act of creating these images forces you to concentrate on what you are trying to remember.* Surprise seeing requires that *you see the images first* before they are described to you. Put the book aside and make your own visual links between the rest of the objects on the list.

Here's how I did it:

Connect **staple** and **Empire State Building**. Remember, don't pay attention to the previous associations. I see a massive number of **staples** coming together to form the **Empire State Building**.

Trust your imagination. Let the images it creates be as real as any reality you have ever seen.

Active images are easier to remember than static ones. Think moving picture instead of snapshot. The images you create are encouraged to move. See these pictures move and see the consequences of this action.

Visualize an arm coming from the **Empire State Building** and **punching** a **diamond** which somehow is suspended in midair at the one hundredth-story level. Connect **diamond** and **butter** by imagining as clearly as you can someone cutting a slab of **butter** with a butter knife, only the **butter** is coated with **diamonds**. That would have an interesting effect on the knife—see the repercussions.

Ever see a **rose** growing out of a stick of **butter**? If not, that's a good link. In the place of **rose** petals, see **light bulbs**. When the **light bulbs** are turned on, instead of a filament inside there's a giant **business card**. Look closely at the **business card**—what constitutes the black letters actually is hundreds of tiny, yet living **typewriters!** Ignoring business card and the rest, you might visualize **toothpaste** squirting out of the **typewriter** every time a key is hit.

Sometimes you will have to distort an object slightly to make it fit the mental image you're creating. For example, a gigantic suitcase is a distorted object. Your imagination is allowed to tamper with the regular makeup of something. Do that as you need to, because it's much more important to have some picture that's close than a picture that is perfect. The original object or information will be what you recall later. There are no permanent rules regarding making memorable images.

Now you've got it! You can go ahead and memorize any list. Try reciting the list; you should be able to recount it perfectly. Pretty amazing, remembering fifteen unrelated objects.

Memory takes confidence, and you should now have that too.

(If you missed an item, don't worry; that only means that your original image wasn't strong or imaginative enough. Go back and re-create a new link. You'll see you can do it with ease. To work, mnemonics requires repetition; you must review any list you want to remember for the long haul. Reviewing through mnemonics is far easier and faster than struggling with rote memorization.)

If you want to get fancy, recite the list backward. And

THE FIRST MEMORY PRINCIPLES

congratulate yourself because it was no problem. Well, you may have this problem: A week from now when you try to forget this "useless" list, you won't be able to. An hour from now this list will be crystal clear, as it will weeks and months into the future. In fact, soon you'll forget the visualizations and associations, the mnemonics, and the list will come to your mind directly.

Some Hints

Let your mind's eye be in control. Think visually, not just verbally, as you are used to doing. Be adventurous in creating your images—let your imagination be cunning and clever. Making objects larger and smaller than life are good techniques; so is creating absurd or humorous situations. Keep your images moving! Action scenes are easier to recall than static pictures. Vulgar and erotic scenes are also easily remembered.

Be actively involved in learning the material—make sure the images are bold and graphic. Rehearse your visualizations. Refresh the mnemonics in your mind's eye several times after you first create your mnemonic. Mnemonics works because it makes you remember, rather than letting you assume you'll remember.

If you have trouble remembering information even after you've repeated the image several times, then that means the image you selected isn't a good one—isn't one that tickles your imagination. Create a new image in its place. And repeat that image from time to time in your mind. Use images from your own background when you can, to give personal details to the mnemonics you create. For example, if you envision the Empire State Building and have been there, see yourself at the entrance. When you create an image for a typewriter, make it a typewriter from *your* past—one that you have particular feelings or association with.

Most memory fails not because we forget, but because we

don't remember in the first place. Memory is more a problem of *attention* than *retention*.

Practice

The following exercise is designed to develop and strengthen your memory skills. Work on them when you have a few minutes to spare. Don't be disappointed if you have difficulty making memory pictures; it's an unfamiliar process and it takes some time to get used to at first, but you'll soon discover that surprise seeing is much faster than rote memorization.

Make sure that these images are clear in your mind. *The clearer the recording, the clearer recall will be.* Memory is a function of how you learn the information. There's an analogy between memorization and television reception. When you have a clear TV picture, you can describe the scene later; when the reception is poor, you can't see or remember much.

Let's review the basic principles of surprise seeing: First, *use images you're familiar with* when you create mnemonic pictures. The greater the detail you can put into the scene, the stronger and longer-lasting the image will be.

Second, *add action.* See things move.

Third, *rely on your intuition.* The images that first appear in your head, whether they are bizarre or ordinary, are the best because the ones that first enter your mind will be the ones you can most easily recall.

Fourth, when you are remembering information, you have to perform triage. *Decide what is important and what's forgettable.* Sometimes you'll have to remember verbatim, but most of the time the gist will suffice. Studying a summary of the material, which you may have to prepare, may be the easiest course to pursue. For example, highlight the facts you'd like to remember in a textbook the first time through. Next time, decide to remember even less, and mark that material in the margin. Don't overexert yourself with unimportant details.

Memorize the following shopping list. Connect only two items at a time.

Pepperidge Farm cookies
Orange juice
Bread
Time magazine
Fish sticks
Cat food
Chicken soup
Perrier water
Mocha Java coffee beans
Garbage bags
Mayonnaise
Tomatoes

Cues, Key Words, and Recall

There are two components to memory: recall and retention. Retaining information is only half the battle because you have to recall it as well. When you have a thought on the tip of your tongue, you *know* that you know the information; it's just that you can't seem to recall it right now. The problem isn't that you never learned the material (try explaining that to the instructor) but that you can't figure out where your brain is storing it.

We must have a **cue** to recall information. There must be a key image, prompt, stimulus, or mnemonic that *makes* us remember. Just about everyone has uttered the phrase, "If you hum a few bars, I'll remember the words." The tune is the **cue** that enables us to locate and repeat the information.

The cue is the connection between the external request for information and the information in your head.

You can have an incredible mass of facts and figures in your memory cells, but without a way of prompting that information to the surface you might as well not know it. You never actually forget; forgetting is a matter of not remembering correctly in the first place. Information that is weakly learned will forever be "on the tip of your tongue." The cue is the thing that you think of first when you want to remember something. It is the image that immediately pops into your head.

For example, the cue in the list you remembered would be **suitcase.** If I asked you to recite the list and you could not remember suitcase, you would have a difficult time recalling the rest of the information. However, if you **link** suitcase to **list** in a way that makes you see the suitcase when you hear the word list, you have created a perfect cue. (You can create that cue by seeing a suitcase drawn on a list—a yellow legal pad will do; or, for a cue, you can imagine the suitcase resting on this page of the book.) Seeing an umbrella smashing a hat will remind you of the hat. You think of the umbrella first, and it reminds you of hat; umbrella is the cue. An example of the cue that most everyone is familiar with: When you can't remember where you put your keys the night before, what most people do is imagine the various places in their house where they *might* have left the keys. You mentally walk through your rooms and see each place until—you hit the spot where the keys are located. Notice that you don't actually see the keys (at first) but rather the place where they are. That place is the cue that lets you see the keys.

If the cue you create is vivid enough, and bears a strong semantic or phonetic relationship to the information you want to learn, you will have no problem with recall. Recall will be automatic. How you remember information—the kind of mnemonics and cues you create—bears directly on how quickly and completely you will be able to recall the information.

The cue is a specific form of the link. Both a cue and a link, or image association, involve connecting the information you want to remember in a meaningful way, in a way *you* are likely to remember. A link can be bizarre, if that works for you or if that's what your mind first conjures, but it doesn't have to be.

The link has to work for you. The connection must be solid in your mind's eye. You must see it. You will know that you have visualized the link when you can ask yourself about particular details and observe them, or when you can manipulate the linked objects. In order to see the link between these objects *they should be touching. Image association functions best when there is a physical connection.* When you visualize a rose growing out of a stick of butter, see the place where the two merge.

Your image association must also make some kind of intuitive sense. Find a way to chain the objects that makes your mind comfortable. If you want to remember balloon and banana, don't think of a balloon resting on top of a banana. That image is better than nothing because the balloon and banana are touching, but a still better image would be to see a banana piercing a balloon. To link a telephone and a Magic Marker, you could replace the telephone handset with the Magic Marker, but a better idea would be to actually see the telephone's keys being colored in one by one.

Link the following objects in each line. The first object is the cue. Where more than two objects are listed, connect only two at a time.

Pizza and tree
FM stereo (the radio signal, not the radio) and hand lotion.
Penguin, pigeon, rooster.
Johnny Carson, rock candy, Jay Leno, a letter opener, Pez
Lightning and snow
The Vietnam war, fork, elevator, a "d" on a typewriter
Metric system and ants
Battery, Mona Lisa, double boiler, love letter
Thoughts, dandelions, a Polaroid camera

Improving Your Visualization and Imagination

Perhaps the key ingredient to a superior memory is the ability to visualize, to turn ordinary, mundane objects and ideas into concrete, memorable *pictures*. The overall process is called visualization.

A lot has been written about the applications of visualization lately. Many books and articles have been published that discuss how visualization can be used to help alleviate pain and disease, enhance creativity, improve mental outlook and help alleviate depression, give insight into ourselves, increase sports performance and, of course, develop an unlimited memory. Not all of these benefits have been completely accepted, especially the medical claims, but there is no doubt that imaging is a powerful and underutilized tool. It is not fully understood. Professional sports teams are using visualization to give them an edge—and it's working. And there is no doubt, as you have already discovered, that creative image making can give you memory abilities that you never dreamed of.

Visualization is a seldom taught skill in the West, and few instructors understand what it involves. It must be taught to be learned, and it must be taught as an adjunct to the verbal skills that are emphasized. You get better at visualization the more you practice.

The key to visualization is that the images you create have to be constructed with pictures. Thinking about the images in words doesn't work. You must exercise your mind's eye and *see* the picture regardless of the kind of information you are learning.

The rest of this chapter is devoted to improving your visual skills.

Radio: The First Step to Mental Images

One exercise you might try if you're having trouble awakening your mind's eye is to listen to radio shows. Almost every community has some station that broadcasts "The Shadow," "A Prairie Home Companion," or some other radio drama. These old-time and not-so-old shows are designed to force you to create pictures as you hear the drama. The writers and actors on the shows have a clear idea about what's going on (what you would see if the drama were on stage), and have designed the show so that you will create that stage in your head. As you listen, let your brain create pictures around the words you hear.

If you were to read the script of one of those shows you would remember less than if you heard it, because people have a harder time remembering information that they read than they hear. Listening forces you to make pictures because it is slower than reading.

Paying Attention

Concentration and focus are basic ingredients of a powerful memory. Only by paying attention to something can you remember it. (That's why it's virtually a waste of time to attend a lecture or try to study when you're sleepy. *You* may be there, but your brain isn't.) If you don't believe that paying attention is vital to a good memory, take the following test:

Which direction does Abraham Lincoln look on a penny?
Which color is on the top of a traffic light?
What appears on the back of a $1 bill?
What appears on the back of a $20 bill?
Does a squirrel's tail curl forward or backward?
Where on the front page does the box with weather information appear in your hometown newspaper?
How many eyelets are on your favorite pair of sneakers?

(The answers to the first five questions are: Right; red, the word ONE in the middle, the great pyramid on the left and the great seal on the right; the White House; backward.)

You should have scored 100 percent in this mini-quiz because you've seen or handled each of the objects mentioned tens of thousands of times. You've especially seen $1 bills and pennies so many times that there should be no doubt in your mind as to exactly what they look like. Yet I'd wager that you scored less than 100 percent on this quiz. (Don't worry, everyone does.) In fact, I wouldn't be surprised if your score was 50 percent or less. Pretty poor, you have to admit; but pretty common, too. The lesson here is that we simply don't remember information we don't concentrate on. Learning by osmosis is rare. You must focus on the information if you want to remember it. You have no choice.

Focusing on the problem at hand requires energy. You must be mentally alert, want to learn the information (if for no other reason than to get it over with) *and* you must be in a good frame of mind. If you are tired you won't form permanent mental connections. If you are in a bad mood, depressed, or anxious, you also will not be able to learn the material. Your mental state is crucial to your ability to pay attention. Memorization, like playing Ultimate Frisbee or squash, or shaving, is an active endeavor. Always keep that in mind. If you can't pay attention, nap now, study later.

Although concentration requires considerable energy, focusing on your work will actually decrease the amount of time you have to study. That's because when you study *and* pay attention, you are making full use of your time. When you study and aren't focusing, you are simply wasting time.

Visualization

If concentration is a lost art, visualization is even rarer. But it's not difficult. You've already begun to enhance your image-making skills through the techniques you've learned so far. But the techniques—surprise seeing, the link, and mimicry—depend so heavily on visualization that it's worthwhile spending a little time developing this skill further. And besides, visualization is fun.

Details

Let's start by focusing on detail, making mental notes about those things we commonly ignore, such as what's on the back of a dollar bill. As you become accustomed to detail you will notice that the world is a great deal more colorful, richer, and interesting than you ever imagined.

Take a look at this page. Notice the running head on the top of the page that mentions the book and chapter title. Notice the page number, how it appears without any dash or other mark around it. Rub your finger over the paper: How would you describe the texture? Put your nose to the paper (it's okay; anyone around you will just think you're napping): How does it smell? And the color? Would you describe the paper as white? Beige? Like an almond or a sandy beach? Notice how the spaces between words and letters actually vary. Flip through the book and you will observe that the odd-numbered pages are always on the right and the even-numbered on the left, as they are with every book.

Feel the book in your hands. Which of the books you own is this heavier than? Lighter? Move your finger over the part of the binding where the pages are glued into the cover. What does it feel like? Can you see the glue that holds the pages in place? Do you notice any aberrations in the binding? What about the color of the glue? Speculate on how the pages, glue, and binding are connected. Look at the book's cover. Where is the author's name located? How does the type the author's name is in compare in size to the type of the title of the book? (I lost that argument.) Is there a Canadian price for the book on the back cover? How many discrete "things" can you identify on the cover? What are their shapes? Colors? Sizes? Locations? What are their purposes?

We could go on for quite a while exploring the details that make up the look of *The Student's Memory Book.* Try the same exercise on other objects. First, your street: Notice how the trees are placed. Pay attention to the shape of the space where the sidewalk meets the street. Look at the buildings, the cars, the color of the asphalt. Next, examine your room. Do the same thing with people's heads. Notice how everyone's ears are shaped differently. Same for their foreheads.

In this exercise (and the next) you are analyzing objects systematically—something most people do not do. Most individuals are terrible witnesses, and if you ever spend time in court you'll see how easy it is for lawyers to demolish a witness's credibility.

Inspect the details of the following objects or others of your own selection:

> A color TV
> Your toothbrush
> A telephone
> Dusk
> The sound of a beer can opening
> A light bulb

Any object can yield vivid, detailed images. You just have to look for them. The more details you are aware of, the easier it will be to memorize that object or information.

The Memorizer as Camera

Pretend you are a camera with a perfect zoom lens. First scan the entire object or scene you are considering. See it and the things around it. Next, let the object fill your entire field of vision, so that you can only see the object you are considering. Now, zero in on a striking detail of the object—whatever fascinates you the most. This exercise will further enhance your ability to see what you usually ignore.

For example, look at a jet aircraft in flight. Notice the clouds around it. Next, focus on just the jet; see the windows, the rubber tip on the nose, where the landing gear is retracted, and the angle of the tail. Zero in on the engine. Pay attention to its size relative to the wing. How is it shaped? What does the shape remind you of? Get in even closer and you will see how the engine is riveted onto the wing (good thing, too). Closer still, and you can make out the individual rivets; a stronger lens and you can see scratches on the rivets.

Zoom in on the following objects:

A pepper grinder on a table
A map of the eastern coastline of the United States
A diamond ring on Raquel Welch's finger
Clark Gable's smile
The Golden Gate Bridge
A snowflake

There's an extra payoff from this exercise. It also enhances your ability to focus on one topic at a time, an essential element for a perfect memory.

Faces

In the chapter on history, you'll uncover quick and simple techniques for learning about events, famous people, and inventions. One of the suggestions offered in that chapter is to find illustrations or photographs of the historical figures you want to learn about. Having a picture of someone makes remembering details about his or her life much easier. But it's not always possible to find pictures of historical figures. When you can't, invent an image for that person in your mind. See the details: the shape of the face; the ears, nose, and mouth; color and style of hair, thickness of the neck, shape of the chin, and so forth. Make a clear picture in your mind.

Invent photographs of these people in your mind's eye. Where you already have a partial image, fill in the blanks with speculative details.

Moses
Thomas Jefferson

Marie Sklodowska Curie
Dag Hammarskjold
Martin Luther King, Jr.

One of the problems most people have with remembering the names that go with faces is that most of us don't pay attention to faces in the first place. Sure, we can recognize our friends and relatives (most of the time), but try these exercises: 1) What color are the eyes of the people who live on your floor? (People you've seen countless times.) 2) Compare your mother's and father's chins. 3) Describe an ear.

Not as easy as it seems.

Information that you want to learn has to receive special attention.

If you want to remember faces, you have to pay attention to them. The following exercise will not only further enhance your ability to perceive details (to see things that others do not see), it will help you learn history and remember people's names.

Pick a part of the face each day for the next week. Every time you see somebody, focus on that part of his or her face. For example, one day examine eyes, the next chins, the following eyebrows. Here's a schedule to follow:

Monday	Eyes
Tuesday	Nose
Wednesday	Lips
Thursday	Cheeks
Friday	Hair line
Saturday	Chin
Sunday	Earlobes

More on Surprise Seeing

Surprise seeing is not a skill you are born with. Although everyone has the ability to see things through their imagination, this talent must be learned. Or, more accurately, relearned, because when we were children we were experts in creative visualization. As children we saw monsters under our bed, imagined pots of gold at the end of the rainbow, conjured images for the Tooth Fairy, looked for hidden pictures in *Highlights* magazine, turned clouds into all sorts of fantasy pictures, and maybe even made up our own constellations. And we really saw these things! Adults don't do that anymore. In fact, being imaginative about our work is frowned upon. We're taught—even forced—to "be logical," to "be realistic," and to "stick to the outline."

But the world does not always lend itself to logic and ordinariness. Mnemonics is a testament to that. So is the story about the high school student who was asked on a test, "Using a barometer, how can you measure the height of an office building?" The student, knowing about barometers and air pressure, thought for a while and wrote this answer: "Drop the barometer from the top of the building and time how long it takes to reach the ground. Because gravity is a constant, affecting all objects equally regardless of mass, using formulas for acceleration and distance, we can calculate the height of the building by how long it takes the barometer to reach the ground."

The student received an F. However, the teacher, being kindly (and probably not wanting to confront irate parents) offered the student another chance to take the test. On the second go-around, the student gave this answer: "Offer the barometer to the building's manager in exchange for the manager's telling you how tall the building is."

You can guess what happened.

There is always more than one way to look at something. How you look at objects can give you new insight into their significance, as well as a better memory.

Let's start by looking at an office building from alternative perspectives. In your mind's eye, walk up to the building and place yourself flush against it. Look straight up along the side. What do you see? Now look at the building from above, as if you are in a helicopter. Suspend yourself in midair and look at the center of the building. Lay the building on its side —do you notice any differences?

Look at a telephone in your mind's eye. Make sure you see a specific telephone, not just think generically about a phone. Examine it from every possible angle. Do you often look at the bottom of a telephone? Look inside the holes in the mouthpiece. Put the phone at improbable angles such as on its side or even upside down.

Let's move from the improbable to the impossible. Your imagination really comes into play as you distort objects and manipulate their size, shape, texture, location, color, sounds, assign them personalities, and otherwise **use your imagination**. Shrink the phone to one fifth of its regular size, but keep the handset normal-sized. Replace the handset with a banana. Make the telephone out of chocolate and eat it. Transform the buttons into eyes. Put the phone on a tree. Levitate the phone and notice that no matter how hard you try, you can't push it down on the desk. Make the telephone alive; when it rings, little hands that are sticking out the sides offer you the handset. Envision the telephone made of solid gold. Next imagine it as composed of water—do you see the waves inside the phone? They become rougher every time the phone rings.

Try the same exercise with the office building. Place the offices on balconies *outside* the windows. Put a giant umbrella on top of the building. Paint the building with polkadots. Replace the bricks with hamburgers. Remove the elevators and place a firefighter's pole in their place (which makes going up very difficult). Distort the building and make it short and squat. Next make it into an arch.

Play with the following objects; see them as they could never be:

> Tennis court
> Pepperoni pizza
> A map of the United States

> Dust
> A computer disk
> Snoopy

During the day, observe ordinary objects and pretend to see them do extraordinary things. You'll find that the more you let your imagination loose on something, the stronger your memory of that thing will be.

The Other Senses

Senses other than sight contribute to memorization. How something sounds, smells, tastes, and feels can enhance your ability to remember and recall information. Advertising jingles that titillate your ear (even if their message is dumb), the smell of leaves burning, and the taste of pancakes are examples of the memory of nonvisual senses. Develop these senses, too, and your memory capabilities will become stronger. Rhyme, for example, not only helps organize information, but stimulates the ear.

Examine through your ear, nose, and sense of touch the following:

> A cat
> A business card
> Chocolate ice cream
> A cloud
> A church bell
> An argument
> Anticipation
> An oral thermometer
> The New York *Times*
> Surf
> A nuclear explosion

Emotional Content

Emotion is another attribute of visualization. When you have feelings toward something, it is not only easier to visualize but it sticks more strongly in your memory. As mentioned earlier, you should have no trouble recalling your happiest and saddest times; being embarrassed and scared are easily relived, too. And so are the memories of the emotions you saw your relatives and friends express. Emotions are strong; they replay our past in living color. They are infinitely memorable; they may be the strongest kind of memory we have.

Impart emotion into the information you want to remember. If you visualize a scene in which someone is drinking a beer, have that person drink out of sadness—see the tears, taste them if you can. If your mnemonic involves someone being hanged, see that person as strong and brave. You can even give emotion to inanimate scenes. You linked a rose to butter by having the rose grow out of a stick of butter. Maybe the butter leaks tears; or somebody picks the rose from the butter and smiles; or the rose has a face that is grinning.

Try to experience that emotion, too. Be sympathetic toward what's occurring in your mnemonics. These feelings will brighten your images.

You can determine what emotion best serves the scene and your memory by observing what is most striking about the scene. Open yourself to the image: *What do you feel?* How is your mind affected? Is this exhilarating, sad, boring, fascinating, scary, or tempting? Whatever you feel is what will be retained longest in your memory.

Link the objects in this list, give emotion to the scene, and describe the motivation behind that emotion:

A cat and dog
A beer bottle, a paperback book, and a radiator
A bowl of soup, an alligator, and a butterfly
Picasso and Tina Turner
A twenty-dollar bill, a street person, and a wristwatch
November, a magnifying glass, and an orange
Heroism and a toaster
Wind rustling the trees and a tuning fork

Action and Movement

Seeing an object in detail is essential to being able to remember it. The more you know about something, the stronger an impression it will make in your mind's eye. But your imagination can go beyond straightforward visualization. By providing movement to your images as you did in the previous examples, you will make them even more memorable. An image with energy is better than a lazy one. You can put movement into any object, even if you normally think of that object as static. If your mnemonic involves a building, see that building swaying in the wind. If the image includes a pear, visualize the pear spinning like a top. Say you want to remember the moon. See the moon bobbing in the sky, or see the man in the moon winking. As long as you do something.

Two gremlins that stand between you and a good memory are familiarity and habit. Images that are easy to conjure and that you see in your mind the same way you see them thousands of times in real life are difficult to remember. Giving movement to your mnemonics will help defeat these gremlins.

Give the following objects action:

> A crayon
> A pizza
> A roll of tape and a fan
> A clothes drier
> An airplane
> Wind
> A diamond ring
> A computer printout and a radiator
> An index card, a diaper, and a sailboat
> A windmill, socks, and neon lights

One Final Thought

You should notice that as you practice imagery three things occur. First, your ability to visualize dramatically improves. Visualization becomes easier, more detailed, and more realistic to your mind's eye. Second, you gain different insights into the objects and concepts you are visualizing. You see things in ways that most people don't; you become freed from having to look at a problem in the only way you were taught. Increased insight is a boost to creativity, and this helps both memory and thinking in general. Third, your ability to concentrate increases with your ability to create pictures in your mind's eye. The more you can focus on the problem at hand, the less time overall you will spend working on that problem.

2

Mimicry

Ah, you may say. Converting solid, tangible objects—like the ones in the previous chapter's examples—into pictures may be easy, but what about remembering information that bears no relationship to the physical world? How do you remember people's and cities' names, foreign-language vocabulary, and scientific words? How do you make a picture out of a word like Toshiba, a name like Haig, the town of Phoenicia, New York, *poulet* (chicken in French), or herogen (a high explosive), the way you can with rose or diamond?

To remember abstract information you will use a technique called **mimicry.** Mimicry involves substituting the informa-

tion you want to learn, such as unintelligible foreign vocabulary, for something you already know.

Remember the absolutely awful children's knock-knock
joke that goes this way:

> Knock-knock.
> Who's there?
> Alaska.
> Alaska who?
> I don't know, but I'll ask her.

After you've taken a moment to groan, consider this: Why is
this joke interesting to children? Because children like to play
with words and sounds they've recently learned. They are
amused by the fact that Alaska can be changed into something with an entirely different meaning, but with roughly the
same sound. "I'll ask her" is an interesting version of Alaska,
but it's more than that. "I'll ask her" is something children
understand, while Alaska is a nonsense sound. In this knock-
knock joke the meaningless sound "Alaska" is translated into
a meaningful expression, "I'll ask her."

By the same system, Toshiba becomes "to ship
a . . ."—and that's exactly what Toshiba does: it ships products. Everything from computers to television sets to print-
ers. **To ship a** is the mimic for **Toshiba**. Notice the *phonetic
connection* between Toshiba and its mimic.

As with the other techniques we've encountered, surprise
seeing and the link, you need to visualize the phrase you've
just created. After you mimic Toshiba's sound, the next step
is to **link** this phrase, "to ship a," with the word's meaning.
You want to create a *semantic connection* as well. See a ship
in a Japanese harbor loading crates of computers and television sets onto it. I'll leave the details of the image up to you,
but make sure that you actually have a detailed image in your
head. Having a Japanese harbor is important, because it
doesn't help to remember Toshiba if you don't know it involves Japan.

You may have noticed that "to ship a" doesn't exactly match Toshiba, which has a "b" sound in it, not a "p" sound. For mimicry to work, you don't have to duplicate the sounds exactly. Just come close enough and your brain will do the rest.

A name example: Alexander Haig, the former Supreme Allied Commander of NATO and former presidential candidate. The name Alexander should remind you of Alexander the Great—picture the Greek leader wearing a modern U.S. Army uniform with 4 stars. So much for the "Alexander" and "general" parts. For "Haig" you might substitute "hag" or "egg." If it's hag, see a hag riding with General Alexander; if you're substituting egg for Haig, put eggs where the stars should be on his uniform.

The two ingredients to mimicry are:

1. Find a word or phrase that mimics the sound of the abstract word or phrase you want to remember, and

2. Try to make the mimicking word or phrase relate semantically to what you're trying to learn. That's not always possible, but it helps secure your memory to construct a semantic bridge between the two.

Somebody told you about Sweet Sue's restaurant in Phoenicia, New York, and about the fantastic pancakes they make there (like the ginger and blueberry pancake that people drive 100 miles from New York City to taste). And you want to remember that Sweet Sue's is located in Phoenicia so that you don't drive to Buffalo, another 400 miles, by mistake. The problem revolves around Phoenicia. Since you want to go to Phoenicia to eat, it makes sense to find a phrase to mimic Phoenicia that has something to do with food. Once you have your mind on food, Phoenicia becomes **fo eat, ya** go to Sweet Sue's. See someone **sewing** (sounds like Sue) in front of a restaurant. Maybe she's even stitching special ingredients into the pancake. See her thread a blueberry. Concentrate on the picture, and include as many related images as you can.

A blue-and-white sign boasting Sweet Sue's name would also be appropriate. (Bear in mind that the expression **fo eat ya** isn't the only way to mimic Phoenicia; alternatives include **phony eats** (are the pancakes really that terrific?) or **phone eats** (can you order out?))

As with all memory techniques, it's best for you to create your own images. Forming personal pictures is an important part of the memory process; memory is never automatic.

More Mimicry

You have to know that *poulet* is chicken in French if you want to be taken seriously at French restaurants. Poulet sounds like **pull leg**, so take a mental snapshot of someone pulling the leg of a chicken.

One of the most powerful nonnuclear explosives is called herogen. Herogen's used for deep-sea oil exploration and to separate spacecraft from booster engines once the boosters run out of fuel and have to be discarded. It is so potent that it can blast through fourteen inches of steel. Mimic herogen with the phrase **hero again**. Picture a hero (the man of steel, if you like) stopping the blast from an explosive with his chest. He does it again and again.

A couple of examples. If you want to remember Iceland and its capital, Reykjavik: A land covered with ice; someone is trying—in vain—to **rake** that land. For India and New Dehli: Imagine **India** ink is smeared all over the front of the **new deli**.

Some Tricks of the Memory Trade

A couple of helpful hints: *Try to incorporate concrete nouns into your mimicry.* Concrete nouns—tangible objects—are far easier to remember than adjectives, verbs, and not-so-concrete nouns. Concrete nouns are objects that you can hold or grasp, such as radiators, pennies, and lima beans. Not-so-concrete nouns are items that you can't grasp, such as oxygen, and excitement.

Second, *see action in your images*. The French word for "duck" is *canard*. The mnemonic mimic could be **can hard**. (Precise pronunciation is not important for our purposes here.) Don't just see a duck half in and half out of a can; actually envision a struggle going on between the chef who's forcing the duck into the can (**can hard**) and the duck who'd rather be elsewhere. Place your images in a situation where there is movement, where images are interacting. Certain kinds of action are easier to remember than others. Some people, for example, find that rough images are more memorable than idyllic scenes. You will quickly discover which types of images suit your memory patterns best.

Third, *use whatever image comes first to your mind*. If the image is a strange one, fine; if it's fairly ordinary, that's okay too. Whatever you first think of when you are trying to remember the foreign language will be what you first think of when you are trying to recall the word later.

Fourth, *if at first you don't succeed, put what you are trying to remember aside*. Focus on something else, and come back to the troublesome word later. Most people who can't create a mnemonic right away have a much easier time the second try. Memorizing information in pieces not only is easier and less stressful, it creates strong images, too.

Fifth, *review your mnemonics*. This is true for every memory technique. Always refresh your mind by going over the mimicked images you've created. Do this a couple of minutes later *and* a couple of hours later *and* a couple of days later. Go over every mnemonic at least three times.

Abstractions

A considerably large amount of information does not lend itself readily to pictures. These are **concepts**, and they are a vital part of every subject's curriculum. The best way to describe a concept is to define it as something that does not produce an image in your mind. The Bill of Rights is an example of a list of concepts. To remember concepts, we have to translate them into specific and vivid images; we have to make the abstract into the real.

Here is where our imagination and creative visualization truly come into play. Mimicry is the mnemonic tool you use to remember abstractions. There are a couple of ways to employ mimicry and transform ideas into images. The first is to make a *phonetic connection*. For example, the concept **good** becomes goods, as in products. The second is to create a *semantic link:* See someone doing **good** deeds, such as helping the homeless. But it's even better to make both a *phonetic and semantic* association between the concept and the image. Thus, "good" becomes "goods" to complete the phonetic link; now imagine that the goods are Red Cross items, for a semantic connection. The Spanish word for chicken, *pollo,* can be remembered by envisioning someone playing **polo** (the phonetic) with **chickens** (the semantic) instead of balls. To remember the concept **voting rights,** turn it into a real image of black people marching into a voting booth. Add detail to the image to reinforce it in your mind: the booth is sparking with electric **volts** and is to the **right** of the voters. To remember the concept **a decline in prices,** imagine a **deck lying** on **prizes;** to add a semantic connection, imagine that the deck is angled downward, **declining,** and that the prizes still have their **price** tags on them.

In the following exercise, convert these concepts into strong, vivid images. Create both phonetic and semantic links between the concepts and the images you create:

> Freedom and disorder
> Breaking up a relationship
> An inflamed eye
> Escape velocity
> The new moon
> Contractual obligation
> Elation
> Curvature of space-time

Education reform
Window of vulnerability
Never again
Rejuvenation

Remembering Names with Mimicry

There are some highly practical and immediate applications for mimicry—remembering names. The same technique that words for remembering foreign-language vocabulary works for remembering first and last names. Many names—Adler, Crawford, Hupping, Makower—for example, don't generate immediate images in your mind, so you have to substitute an English word or phrase for the sound.

Let's look at the first five vice presidents of the United States (two of whom became President). They are: John Adams, Thomas Jefferson, Aaron Burr, George Clinton, and Elbridge Gerry. To remember John Adams, see an image of an **atom** (preferably the *first* atom on the periodic table, hydrogen) swirling around in a **john**. For Thomas Jefferson, you have several options. Thomas can be **Tom** Thumb, **Thomas'** English Muffins, or a **tom**-tom. Link one of these images to a mimic of Jefferson: You could use **heifer's son**, or **Joffrey Ballet**. Aaron Burr, one of the lesser-known early vice presidents, is also an easy name to learn: envision an **arrow** that has shot a **burr**. For George in George Clinton, use **gorge** and link that to **clipped on** (to the White House). Finally, a mnemonic for Elbridge Gerry. Visualize a **bridge** in the shape of an **L jeering**.

If you can locate pictures of these vice presidents, link the mimicry you've created to their pictures. Remembering names works best when you have a specific image to work with.

Patterns and Organization

The brain loves to organize. It likes to establish categories, to make neat piles of information and discover patterns. The greater the organization you can impose on the information you want to know, the easier it will be to memorize that information *and the stronger your memory will be.* Fortunately, any kind of information can be organized: patterns come in every flavor. Rhyme, size, direction, analogies (Jimmy Carter reminds me of my uncle), differences, and bunching similar objects together are examples of ways information can be organized.

Mimicry works precisely because the brain recognizes and remembers patterns. Mimicry is based on the principle of organization.

Say you have the following objects to remember:

> Newspaper
> Coffee
> Flowers
> Cat
> Cookbook
> CBS Evening News

There are several patterns here. Pattern number 1: You could group these objects into two categories: Those that start with a **C** and those that don't. You could call this an alphabetical pattern. Pattern number 2: Reading the **newspaper,** drinking **coffee,** and feeding the **cat** are all morning activities; buying **flowers** for your girlfriend, using the **cookbook,** and watching the **CBS Evening News** are evening events. Pattern number 2 is a schedule pattern.

Once you put information into a category, all of a sudden the information is twice as easy to remember. Some kind of organization is necessary for everything you want to remember.

Organization can occur in many different ways because there are unlimited similarities and other relationships between objects that can be used to classify them.

When you organize information you are forming *links* (image association), sometimes also called **chunking.** One of the reasons linking enhances memory, besides creating visual impressions of the information, is that it frequently reduces the number of segments of information you must remember. When you link fifteen objects together as you did in Chapter 1, you have to remember only one—the first, **the** cue that prompts you to recall the rest of the list—rather than all fifteen items. The combined mental image may be more complex than before, but there is only one piece of information to remember.

No predetermined pattern or organization is right or wrong. Whatever structure *your* mind creates is the appropriate pattern. Each set of information to be remembered may require a different kind of organization. Unlike most subjects you study, with mnemonics the only major rule is *use what works best for you.*

Information that doesn't make sense in the form in which it's first presented to you may be comprehensible when you organize it. For example, if you try to remember **ihadarelaxingeveningwithpeggylastnight** you could encounter some problems. If you organize the information a little differently like this:

> i
> had
> a
> relaxing
> evening
> with
> peggy
> last
> night

the information is easier to remember. Now, if you make it look like this, **I had a relaxing evening with Peggy last night** it becomes still easier. Finally, if you add mental snapshots of last night that include you and Peggy, then remembering the phrase becomes no problem at all.

Let's look at two other kinds of organization, rhyme and acronyms.

Rhyme

Rhyme is a powerful mnemonic tool because it puts information into strong patterns and because it stimulates our senses. Many complex or abstract sets of information can be organized into a rhyme or a jingle. Countless examples abound. To remember which months have thirty-one or thirty days remember the rhyme:

> Thirty days hath September,
> April, June and November.
> All the rest have thirty-one
> Excepting February alone.

This information is far easier to remember in rhyme than by using a rote system.

An admonition for children:

> Ice skating is nice skating
> but here's some advice about
> ice skating.
> Never skate where the ice is
> thin.
> Thin ice will crack and you'll
> fall right in.

We tend *never* to forget these rhymes.

A rule of spelling:

> I before e,
> Except after c,
> Or when sounded like a
> As in "neighbor" or "weigh."

Our first completely memorized historical fact:

> In fourteen hundred ninety-two,
> Columbus sailed the ocean blue.

Many Americans rely on this rhyme to remember when

Columbus discovered America. And why not? It's much easier to recall than the date alone, 1492.

More history—the end of the Civil War, via rhyme:
When the Union did survive,
'Twas eighteen hundred sixty-five.
Finally, how to turn a screw:
Righty tighty,*
Lefty loosey.
Many kinds of information can be converted into rhyme. You'll probably have a good time making your own.

Acronyms

Acronyms are another way of categorizing information. To create a mnemonic acronym, string the first letter of each word in the list of things you want to remember and turn those letters into a word, phrase, or other meaningful image. For example, the colors of the rainbow (the spectrum) are

red orange yellow green blue indigo violet

This information becomes: **Roy G. Biv**, who gives us the colors in their correct order.

More on the Cue (and Mimicry)

The cue, introduced in the previous chapter, is among the most important elements in mnemonics. You must have a prompt that enables you to recall the information you've memorized. The cue is the image that brings forth the memorized information. It is a visual stimulus. Here are some examples of the cue applied to mimicry. To remember the Spanish word for chicken, you see chickens being pushed around by polo sticks, and that rings a bell: "chicken" in Spanish is *pollo*. The cue is chickens being batted around by **polo** sticks. If you want to remember that fertilization takes place in the Fallopian tubes, you would see an **egg** rolling

---

* Lynn Rhinehart told me this mnemonic.

over a waterfall into a tube. Egg, the cue, generates the rest of the picture.

The image that is your mnemonic cue should be linked as closely as possible to both the information you want to remember and the actual thing itself. Chickens being hit by polo sticks is a good cue because the image reminds you that there's a phonetic resemblance lurking here. Egg is a good cue when you want to remember where fertilization occurs because when you hear the word fertilization, you are apt to think or see "egg." That's a semantic link. Strong cues help create potent images that let you recall information in two directions. When asked what *pollo* means, you are likely to think, *"pollo, pollo, pollo,* ah, **polo**," then see a polo game being played with a chicken.

Some Important Exercises

Memorize the following information using the techniques you've learned so far: surprise seeing, the link, and mimicry. Memorize the information along with whatever details you think are pertinent to the information or help you remember what you need to know.

Information to Remember	*Additional Details*
Juan Vicente Gómez	Former dictator of Venezuela
hygrometer	An instrument used to determine relative humidity, to measure the moisture content of gases.
Dr. Michael Zasloff, discoverer of magainins	Magainins are a powerful antibiotic derived from the African clawed frog.

First Interlude

objects in extraordinary ways. Change size, shape, location, even function of things you see during the day.
Impose one friend's ears or hair on another friend's
fac.

Metaknowledge is knowledge about knowledge. When
you are studying biology or English literature, you're
acquiring knowledge about those subjects. But when
you learn mnemonics you are acquiring metaknowledge. Mnemonics teaches you how to learn other subjects. It's both a higher form of knowledge, because
once you know memory systems you can remember any
kind of information, and a more basic kind of knowledge, because mnemonics forms the foundation for
learning everything else.

Take a break from this book for a while. Rest and
play are vital aspects of learning, as important as studying. Rest and play rejuvenate the body, give the subconscious time to mull over what you've learned, relieve
stress and anxiety, and give you a chance to look at
things later in different ways.

But before you take a break, think about the following three points:

1. Organizing information into manageable categories speeds memorization and creates longer-lasting images. As you read new material or hear a lecture, think
about how the facts could be chunked together according to shapes, sounds, similar first letters, similar mo-
tives, differences, and analogies (what the information
reminds you of).

2. Use images and categories that have personal significance for you, when you can. Images created out of
objects that you once owned, held, or saw are more

memorable than those conjured purely by your imagination.

3. Think in pictures. Have fun looking at ordinary objects in extraordinary ways. Change size, shape, location, even function of things you see during the day. Impose one friend's ears or hair on another friend's face.

3

Remembering Numbers

(And Learning the Bill of Rights at the Same Time)

Numbers are among the most difficult types of information to remember. Designed to represent everything from quantities of apples to π (pi), they are the ultimate abstractions. Numbers vanish quickly from our minds. Numbers don't conjure any pretty pictures in your mind, they don't easily connect with any already remembered information. Most people remember digits for only a few seconds; and most people, when they need to remember important numbers, have to repeat these numbers rapidly over and over and over and over until they find a pen. And heaven forbid the pen should be out of ink.

Trying to remember numbers can be a frustrating task. But

that's only when you try to memorize digits through rote memorization. Applying memory techniques to numbers can make memorizing numbers easy and, what's more important, permanent.

Numbers come in two kinds. First are numbered items in lists. You may have no trouble remembering the first four items on a list but the moment you try to memorize the fifth, details one through four vanish from your head. The second kind involves numbers in sets of seemingly random digits, like phone numbers, dates, mathematical constants, and map coordinates.

The Top Ten System

Let's tackle the first type. Like most of the techniques examined in this book, remembering lists is an enjoyable process. Relax and read. There are many categories of information that come in groups of ten (or fewer). The Bill of Rights is one; the Ten Commandments another; the five continents; the Ten Things You Need to Know to Pass This Exam (perhaps the most common). The reason we have trouble remembering what we hear is that we have no way of filing information for easy recall. We forget because we have no *organizing system*. An analogy would be a library without a Dewey Decimal or Library of Congress catalog system. Finding the book you want would be almost impossible. But with an organizing system, locating a book (if it's there) is a straightforward task. The same holds true for memory: with a simple organizing system, we can remember any amount of information—and recall it instantly.

The Top Ten system is a way of placing the information in preorganized categories. Viva the organization!

Each number, 1 through 10, can be represented by a picture. These number-pictures become our filing system. In order to make the filing system as easy as possible to learn, the pictures that represent these numbers look like the numbers themselves. The number 1 is a pen, 2 is a swan, a 3 looks like

a bird in flight, and a 4 is a sailboat. Remembering the filing
system is like a children's game. These pictures serve as **cues**
for the information you want to remember. Here's the complete list of number pictures for the Top Ten system:

1	pen
2	swan
3	bird
4	sailboat
5	hook
6	golf club
7	cliff
8	snowman
9	lollipop
10	bat and ball

Sketch a picture of this image next to each number. It
doesn't matter whether you can draw or not; the process of
creating the picture will be sufficient for you to know which
picture goes with what number.

It takes about three minutes to connect the pictures with
the numbers permanently and once you've done that you've
created a filing system that can be used for a myriad of purposes.

And that's about all you need to do to be able to remember
lists of up to ten items. Of course there's a little more involved in the process, such as the information you want to
recall. The final step is to connect the information to the
number. This is accomplished by **linking** the data to the number. For example, pretend you're going shopping and you
need to purchase three items: eggs, chocolate, and milk. To
remember the first item, eggs, link eggs to a pen. Make a
picture involving a pen and an egg, perhaps a pen jabbed into
a egg that causes the yolk to spill out. To remember the
second item, connect a swan and chocolate this way: a snow-
white swan covered with messy, melted chocolate. Finally,
envision a bird drinking milk like a cat. When you want to

remember your list, simply reverse the process. If it's the second item you need to remember, first think of a swan, because it represents the number 2. If your original picture is strong enough, you'll immediately visualize the swan covered in chocolate and know that you have to pick up chocolate.

Frequently, though, the information that has to be remembered for exams is abstract ideas rather than concrete objects like shopping lists. To internalize lists of abstract information, you need to use a slightly different method. But it's no more difficult to memorize lists of abstract items than it is to learn any other information.

Let's go through the entire list of ten, using the Bill of Rights as an example. Most people, including many lawyers, don't know the first ten Amendments to the Constitution, even though they form the foundation of our liberties. So while you're practicing this system, you might as well learn the Bill of Rights once and for all.*

The First Amendment says that Congress shall make no law establishing a religion, or restricting freedom of speech or of the press, or the right to assemble. To remember that this is the First Amendment, make a picture linking these notions with a **pen.** Turn the abstract concepts—freedom of the press, religion and assembly—into a concrete picture. See pens, plenty of pens **assembled** together, battling swords in front of a church, synagogue, or mosque. The pens represent speech and the press. The pens are trying to prevent the swords from entering the church. Make an extra-vivid picture in your mind's eye: See the action, hear the clanging of swords and pens. Notice somebody peering out from the church, if you want, or see the grass on which the pens and swords are fighting sway in the wind. You can even see a sword break through the line of pens and—almost—burst into the building. Concentrate on the picture. In this scene, the pen stands for the concept of freedom of press, and the fact that there

---

* The Amendments contain more detail than we are covering here. Once you've memorized the basics of the Bill of Rights, you can fill in the details on your own.

are a multitude of pens assembled represents the right to assemble. Finally, because the scene takes place in front of a religious institution, we relate the picture to freedom of religion.

What we have done is translate abstract concepts into concrete images through the powerful memory technique of **surprise seeing**. Pictures are much easier to remember than theoretical legal principles, and those pictures that involve action, color, and strange or surreal events such as turning pens into soldiers of sorts are the most easily remembered pictures. In other words, the more entertaining the picture, the more memorable. The scenes we've created are linked to the number-picture filing system in a way that makes sense for the particular scene. In the case of the First Amendment, we're lucky because the pen represents both the number 1 and the concept of freedom of the press.

Now for the Second Amendment, which says "the right of the people to keep and bear arms, shall not be infringed." Imagine a swan family (the number 2), swimming peacefully along a country lake with machine guns (representing "right to bear arms") slung over their shoulders. Again, actually visualize the scene in your mind's eye. (One of my students suggested an alternative image: a man machine-gunning the swans as they float alone. I prefer the first picture, but if this one is more striking to you, by all means use it.) The surprising sight of swans with machine guns would never exist in the real world; because of this it's easy to remember the link between the designated image for the number 2, the swan, and arms.

There are two processes involved here. The first is **mimicking** the abstraction you want to know with a concrete image. Substitute one for the other. The second process involves **linking** this image to the number picture, our file system. That's all.

The Third Amendment prohibits quartering troops in homes during peacetime. (In prerevolutionary days this was a vital issue because the Crown, by keeping troops in people's homes, could effectively control the population. It's difficult to rebel when you have a soldier as a roommate.) Picture a soldier flying into a house on top of a giant bird (the number 3). *That* image should do the trick. Later when you try to recall what the Third Amendment says you'll think of a bird and instantly this image will fly into your head. And if someone asks you "Which amendment pertains to quartering troops in homes during peacetime?" your mind will conjure a house, a soldier—then you'll see the soldier on a bird: voilà—the Third Amendment.

The Fourth Amendment to the Constitution of the United States protects us against unreasonable "searches and seizures." Linking search and seizure to "sailboat" (the number 4) takes no time at all: Visualize the crew of a Coast Guard vessel seizing a recreational sailboat. Alternatively, see two children playing with a toy sailboat in a lake: One of them seizes the boat.

Although I'm providing specific scenes (or stories, if you prefer) for each Amendment, it's always best if you create your own images. The act of composing your own pictures is a tremendous boost to memorizing the Bill of Rights—or anything. As your brain focuses on devising a creative image for what you want to learn, it is vigorously involved in the process of memorizing that information. Impelling your mind to look at information in unique ways is a crucial aspect of memorization. In surprise seeing, you should create the surprise.

After you read about the next six amendments, take a few minutes to develop your own images before looking at the ones I've created. Your memory of the Bill of Rights will be that much stronger.

The Fifth Amendment is among the most important, and the most complicated. It says that a grand jury indictment is required in capital crimes, no person shall be tried for the same crime twice (put in "double jeopardy"), no one shall be compelled to testify against himself, that no one shall be "deprived of life, liberty, or property, without due process of law," and finally, that private property shall not be taken for public use without "just compensation." (This last section explains why states can appropriate property to build highways and other projects.) All right, here is the memory part. Take the hook, which stands for the number 5. Imagine a **grand** piano attached to the hook; only sitting on the bench and playing the piano together is an entire **jury**. Next, attached to the same hook are two **Jeopardy** game boards. If you look upward, you'll see that the hook is attached to the courtroom stand that witnesses **testify** in; if that part of the scene isn't enough to remind you of the prohibition against requiring you to testify against yourself, visualize somebody in that stand testifying in front of a mirror—that will remind you. Next, balance the scales of liberty—which as we know stand for justice (due process)—on the hook. Finally, add the notion of just compensation to the scene by putting money on one side of the scale and your house (or maybe a Monopoly house) on the other side. If you've used my image instead of creating your own, go over it a couple of times more in your mind—really see the picture.

The Sixth Amendment guarantees every criminal defendant the rights to a speedy and public trial, to trial by an impartial jury (of his peers) in the locality where the crime was committed, to be confronted by the witnesses against him, and to be defended by counsel. This amendment leads to one of my favorite scenes. See a group of lawyers, dressed crisply in their gray pinstriped suits, playing golf. (The golf club looks like the number six—remember?) Suddenly they put the clubs down and race to a **court** of law, with a basketball hoop inside, and continue their physical activity (still dressed in suits, naturally). In the jury box are farmers, all dressed identically, wearing the same high school T-shirt, in fact; they are **peering** at a woman in the witness stand, also wearing the same T-shirt. Wearing the same shirt reinforces the notion that the jury and the accused are peers. Make the image of the woman as detailed as possible: Is she young? Old? In handcuffs? What color is her hair? How does she move her head and arms? To translate the right to be confronted by witnesses against you, have the woman stare into the eyes of a face that is floating freely in the air; the face is attached to a torso and this apparition's arm is pointing a finger toward the accused. (An alternative image involves putting **pears**—with noses, eyes, ears, and other facial parts —in the jury box: pears sound like peers; the surprise of a specific image, pears, for the concept, peers, will remind you that it's a jury of peers. The possible images are as varied as your imagination; use what works best for you.)

It may feel as if the scenes we have created for some of the Amendments are contrived, at the very least, or even extreme —especially the previous three amendments. But it only seems this way because you've never applied these techniques before. Memory skills are a little like learning how to multiply: At first multiplication seemed unusual and impossible; now it's a part of your everyday life. But as cumbersome as these scenes may appear (and that feeling will pass as you use your newfound memory skills), using these techniques is a lot easier, quicker, and more permanent than memorizing the Bill of Rights by rote (if you could).

Now is a good time quickly to review the first six amendments. If this is the first time you've used memory techniques, give your brain a chance to get used to this new way of learning. Let your mind see the visual connections between the substance of the amendments and the number pictures once more. Take a minute or two, then continue.

The Seventh Amendment gives the right to a jury trial for all suits involving twenty dollars or more. Picture a jury in its box, balanced precariously on the edge of a cliff (for the number 7): Each member of the jury is waving a twenty-dollar bill in his or her hand.

The Eighth Amendment prohibits cruel and unusual punishment and bars requiring excessive bail. Picture a snowman (the number 8) strapped in an electric chair, only the chair is constructed not out of metal, but bales (**bails**) of hay. Now you'll have no trouble remembering the Eighth Amendment.

The Ninth Amendment to the Constitution says: The enumeration in the Constitution of certain rights "shall not be construed to deny or disparage others retained by the people." This means that just because a particular right isn't mentioned in the Constitution doesn't mean it does not exist. Picture a lollipop (9) with arms, swinging a punch with its **right** arm—that's all you need to do to turn a very abstract concept into concrete memory. It is indeed amazing that all you have to do to remember an abstract thought is make a picture.

The Tenth Amendment of the Bill of Rights is the "states' rights" amendment—it delegates powers that are not specifically mentioned or prohibited to the states, or the people. Linking the concept of states' rights with a bat and ball for the number 10 should almost be facile: See a baseball field, and pay particular attention to the bases. Watch the batter hit the ball (to right field, if you want); instead of the bases, there are **steaks**, which sounds close enough to states—mimicry again. (The steaks can even resemble bases.) Alternatively, your mind's eye could conjure the picture of a batter hitting steaks instead of a ball. The steaks are being hit toward **people**. Still another alternative is to imagine that the playing field is actually a map of the United States, and the game being played involves hitting balls to particular states.

That's the Bill of Rights. Granted, we traveled an unusual course to memorize the Bill of Rights, and it probably took a little longer to review them than if you were simply to read the first ten amendments. But that's only because this is the first time you've used these techniques. After a while, these techniques will seem as natural as . . . well, rote memorization. But there's a tremendous difference between trying to remember the Bill of Rights by rote versus using memory skills: You now will know the Bill of Rights forever. This system can be used to remember any kind of information. If you want to look attentive during a lecture, instead of taking notes just link the professor's most important points to the number-pictures 1 to 10. Chances are that no instructor will say more than ten things per hour that are worth remembering. You can also use the number-picture system while you're reading. When it's inconvenient to take notes, or if your pen should decide to go on strike, just tie the key information to the number pictures. In fact, there's an advantage to memorizing information over taking notes—you don't have to work at remembering it later.

Learning Digits: Mathematical Constants, Phone Numbers, Distances, and Other Numerical Information

The second system for remembering numbers works very differently. In fact, the system we're going to use is unique in this book in that it is the only technique you actually have to memorize. While all the other memory systems are freewheeling, the digit system is much more structured.

If this sounds potentially onerous, it's not. To remember numbers, you have to learn only ten mnemonics—one for each digit, 0 to 9. It shouldn't take more than fifteen minutes. And that's not too bad, considering that this system will enable you to learn and remember an infinite combination of digits—everything from telephone numbers to dates to mountain heights to distances between stars. The system works by representing each digit with a sound. The sounds are then strung together to form words, and the words, as you're already discovered, can be quickly transformed into memorable pictures.

In this system, there is a direct relation between numbers and sounds. (Some digits can be depicted by more than one sound.) For example, 1 is the sound **t** or **d**. A 2 is the sound **n**.

Remember, each number is represented by a phoneme, not a letter; it's the sounds that are important.

The sounds that represent consonants are as follows:

1	t/d
2	n
3	m
4	r
5	l
6	sh/ch
7	k/hard g (as in golf)
8	f/v/th
9	p/b
0	z/s

Consonants retain their sound much more consistently than vowels do in English, which is why consonants are the constants for digits. Sounds not represented on this list such as w, h, y, soft g, and j have no numerical value. But x *can* have value depending on how it sounds. X can sound like k as in hex, or z, as in xylophone. Keep in mind that this is a phonetic system.

Also remember that this system takes considerable practice if you want to become accomplished at it. It is worth it.

Because this entire book is based on the philosophy that rote memorization isn't necessary, even in the one instance where rote memorization seems to be required you can use mnemonics to learn the correspondence between digits and sounds. Here is the shortcut:

1 has a single downstroke and so does a **t**.

2 looks like an **n** turned on its side.

3 looks like an **m** turned on its side, or the Roman numeral III.

4 ends in **r**.

5—well, if you open your hand and spread your five fingers,

the spread between the thumb and first finger looks like an
l.

6 looks like a broom, and brooms are used to brush.

7 is the backside of a k.

8 is curved like an f.

9 is the mirror image of a p.

Finally, an 0 is a zer0.

That's it. As you can tell, it's not going to be hard to learn
this system. Although this technique was developed over a
century ago, it has withstood advances in computer technol-
ogy and other modern data storage systems: it is the most
effective system for remembering numbers ever devised. Unlike computers, this system doesn't suffer from electrical
power failures or disk crashes. And it's completely portable.

Now for the application.

If you want to memorize the area code for Woodstock,
New York, 914, you would convert these digits into their
respective sounds:

9 equals p or b

1 equals t

4 equals r

Turn these consonants into a word by mixing them with
vowels: Potter is an excellent word. (Remember double letters count as a single sound.)

Next link potter to Woodstock. Envision a potter sitting in
the middle of the Woodstock festival or in the middle of the
Woodstock town center, if you know what the town looks
like. (Although the festival wasn't held in the town itself,
that's not relevant to our mnemonic.) Alternatively, envision
everyone in Woodstock—or at the festival—as a potter.

When you want to recall the area code, you will think
"Woodstock," then see the potter, then convert potter to 914.

Two quick examples: 402 is raisin; 8052 is Vaseline.

Say you want to remember how many votes Rutherford B.

Hayes received when he won the presidential election in 1876: 4,033,768. That's the kind of number that an ordinary person (one who doesn't know mnemonics) would recall for a mere twenty seconds, if that. First, translate that figure into a phrase:

4	is a	r
0	is a	s or z
3	is a	m
3	is a	m
7	is a	k
8	is a	f or v
6	is a	sh or ch
8	is a	f or v

4,033,768 becomes "rose mom cave shave." (Remember, it's the sounds that count, not the letters.) Although this is a fairly nonsensical-sounding phrase, rose mom cave shave, it's easy to link with Rutherford Hayes. Picture the following scene occurring in a cave (where if you like, people are voting): "Mom" (yours or Hayes's) picking a rose from the President's ear while he is shaving off the hay that's grown on his face. You remember President Hayes because what other President has hay growing on his face? To remember the number of votes that President Hayes received, turn the picture "rose mom cave shave" back into numbers by reversing the process.

As with the other memory systems, remembering numbers will take a while to get used to. As awkward as it may seem in the beginning, there is no better way to remember long sets of digits. Although it may have taken a couple of minutes for you to remember rose mom cave shave, it probably would have been *impossible* for you to learn 4,033,768 for the long haul any other way.

A couple of rules to keep in mind. When forming words, rely only on the sounds that these letters stand for, not the letters themselves. So you would ignore double letters if they produce a single sound. The number 514 could become later; 5114 would not be le*tt*er (it could be "lead tear").

Let's try another example. Perhaps you have to know when the Dutch artist Gerrit van Honthorst was born—1590 —and when he died—1656.

To remember the date 1590, make pictures out of the sounds t/d–l–p/b–z/s which become **tall bass**. A **tall bass** (fish) giving birth to the Dutch paint boy, or the painter painting a **tall bass** in a crib would work.* Let your imagination roam and it will select the most appropriately memorable image. A six-foot-tall fish, as strange as it may be, easily comes into my head. Mr. van Honthorst died in 1656, which translates to **d ch l sh**. Visualize the Dutch paint boy lying dead in a **ditch** with a **leash** around his neck.

The telephone number for the United States Capitol is 202-224-3121; it's the number you use to call any member of Congress. 202 becomes **niacin,** which you can use for any phone number beginning with 202. (Still another alternative is that you might simply know that the U.S. Capitol will be in Washington, D.C., and the 202 area code. It's never worthwhile using these systems to remember information you already have in cerebral storage; that's simply a waste of time.) The rest of the phone number can be converted into **nun ram TNT.** See the image of a nun ramming into a block of TNT (the habit's wimple scoops up the TNT) to get it away from the U.S. Capitol Building. If it helps, throw in the picture of a telephone, either in the nun's hand or on top of the Capitol.

The area of Shenandoah National Park is 194,826 acres. That number is easily converted into **tuber van ouch.** Picture a tuber (someone tubing down a river) colliding with a van. The only possible outcome is for the tuber to yell, "OUCH!"

ϵ, an irrational number that is the base of natural logarithms and is the limit of the mathematical expression $(1 + 1/n)^n$ and which is approximately equal to 2.71828, can

* If you're concerned about confusing van Honthorst with other Dutch painters, particularly Rembrandt, connect the crib to a **vane** (for van).

also be remembered using this system. Try necktie vine hive. Now visualize a log (the log stands for є, log) wearing a necktie.

Numbers are used in a variety of circumstances. If you want to remember that Monroe was the fifth President of the United States, you would see a **man** rowing (Monroe) in hail in a pool in front of the White House. Once you've mastered this system, you will realize that it has infinite uses.

By transposing the process, turning the words that are conjured by these images back into numerals, you will be able to recall the dates you need to know.

You don't always have to construct a picture, either. A phrase is easier to remember than abstract numbers, and the phrase may be all you need to learn. This is particularly true if you want to remember the digits for only a little while.

As with the other memory systems developed in this book, remembering numbers becomes easier the more you use it. I found that remembering the telephone numbers that were given to me was the most enjoyable application of this technique—it always impressed people who *knew* that I hadn't written their number down.

Beyond the Top Ten

Earlier in this chapter you learned the Top Ten system. The Top Ten's limitation is that it only goes to 10. If you want to remember lists that are up to 100 items long, you can use the mnemonic images for numbers 11 to 100. Link the information you want to remember to the mnemonics for 1 to 100.

1 to 101

If you know images for the first 101 digits, you can link these images to remember any length number, instead of creating a new image for every new number you have to remember. Whether it's better to link the images for 1 to 101 or make an original image to remember a new number depends on the circumstances and you.

Here are the first 101 numbers:

1	hat (the h, along with the w and g, has no meaning in this system)
2	U.N., hen
3	ham
4	hair, wire
5	hell, hail, or owl
6	ash, shoe
7	key
8	hive
9	paw
10	dice
11	toad
12	tuna
13	tummy, dome
14	door
15	towel
16	tushy, dish
17	talk (the l is silent and silent letters don't count)
18	tough (the gh sounds f, and it's the sound, not the letter, that matters)
19	tab
20	nose
21	nut (or net, nude)
22	nun
23	name
24	near (or nowhere, owner)
25	noël
26	nosh (as in to snack)
27	nuke (noxious would be 270)
28	knife

29	knob
30	mows
31	moat
32	moan (or mane)
33	mime
34	mare
35	mule
36	mush
37	mike
38	move
39	mop
40	rose
41	rut
42	rain
43	ram
44	roar
45	rail
46	rash (or roach)
47	rock
48	rave
49	rob (or robe)
50	lazy (or loss, Louis—if you know one, laws)
51	light
52	lane
53	lamb
54	lure
55	lily
56	leash
57	leak
58	leaf
59	robe
60	chase (chastise equals 6010)
61	shot
62	chin
63	chime

64   chair
65   shawl
66   cha-cha (the dance)
67   choke (chocolate would be 6751 in
        case you want to know now)
68   shave
69   chop
70   cozy
71   kite
72   can (Canada is 721)
73   comb
74   car
75   kill
76   cash (and catch is 716)
77   kooky
78   cave
79   cap
80   vase
81   fat
82   fan
83   foam (family stands for 835)
84   fairy
85   foil
86   fish
87   fake
88   fife
89   VIP (or veep)
90   booze
91   boat
92   bone (bona fide equals 9281)
93   poem
94   pour
95   pole
96   push (or bush)
97   poke (or pike)
98   pave (and pavement is 98321)

99	pop
100	teases
101	test

And so on.

Alternative Methods to Remembering Numbers

There's yet another system you can use to remember numbers that involves relating the number to something else. Everyone knows that π is approximately 3.14. But it probably took a while to learn that, and the first time you either were not certain of the answer, or you scribbled down 3.14 as quickly as possible before the digits passed into neuron oblivion. But an easier way to remember that π is 3.14 is to turn 3.14 into a price: $3.14. It's perfectly reasonable that a pie would cost $3.14.

Substituting prices for numbers is the fastest way to remember information that comes in the form of digits. It may not be as long-lasting as using number pictures, but it can let you recall information for a great deal longer than you would be able to by simply repeating the number over and over again. Converting numbers to prices works because prices are easy to remember. Put differently, our brains are accustomed to remembering prices. We deal with prices all the time. Because it is a form in which we are accustomed to seeing numbers, our minds don't shriek at prices, but rather readily accept them.

Let's say you want to remember the Washington, D.C., address 2895 Ordway Street. 2895 may be tough, but when converted to $28.95 which is **ordinary** (sounds like Ordway), it shouldn't be difficult to remember at all. A couple more examples: John Masefield, an English poet, was born in 1878. 1878 becomes $18.78; if you want to complete the picture, see a baseball **field** with **maces** instead of bases—and of course there's someone in the field reading poetry. The *Mayflower* landed at Plymouth in 1620. If you pause for a few seconds,

$16.20 could be what the Pilgrims were charged to cross the Atlantic.

After a while, it can become difficult not to think of numbers in terms of prices.

Numbers and You

There are enough events in your own life to create an almost infinite number of mnemonic files for remembering numbers. These files don't have to be numbers, specifically, but can relate to numbers. For example, say you have to remember the zip code 20036—downtown Washington, D.C. Break the zip code into meaningful components: 20 may not be meaningful, but chances are that something occurred while you were twenty that you can create a picture with. Perhaps you bought your first car when you were twenty—make a vivid image of that and **place your car in downtown Washington, D.C.** As for the rest of the zip code, 036: When you were zero, you weren't born yet. Picture you—as a fetus —in your car. When you were three you rode a tricycle, when you were six you entered first grade. Of course, not all numbers may be so coincidentally easy to learn, but surprisingly many are.

Making Patterns

There are still other ways to learn numbers. Although numbers seem annoyingly random, they aren't always. Patterns of digits frequently repeat, and you can use this repetition to your advantage. Think of all the numbers that are indelibly etched in your brain cells: Your address, phone number (and the numbers of friends), Social Security number, weight, the speed limit, distance between the Atlantic and Pacific coasts, the year we landed on the moon, your birth year, the year when the next presidential election will be held. When you have a number to memorize, try to match that number, or part of it, with a number you already know. Pi (π) again: When extended several more digits, π is

3.141592. It's easy: A pie cost $3.14 in 1592. Perhaps you meet someone at a party who gives you her phone number. You may not want to immediately convert those digits into sounds and then make a picture while you're trying to display your brilliant conversational skills. If her number is 227-1138, then you should have no trouble instantly remembering that number: 22 may be your age or her age; 7 is lucky (and you are lucky that she gave you her number); 1138, you may happen to know is part of the title of a now-famous science fiction film, THX 1138.

Another phone number example: 438-5159. If 438 is hard to match with numbers you already know, don't worry about the first three digits. You don't always need to find a way to learn all the digits in a number mnemonically; your brain actually has the ability to remember some things on its own. (Telephone exchanges can also be easily figured out later.) If you're from New York City you know that 51 and 59 are adjacent stops on the Lexington Avenue IRT. If you're not from New York City, then you can use yet another system: **number patterns**. 5159 fits into a logical equation: $5 - 1 + 5 = 9$.

Another phone number example: 246-1418. Notice the pattern among the first three digits: 2 plus 4 is 6. In the last four digits: 4 doubled is 8; the two 1s are place markers to separate the four from the eight.

Patterns are more common than most people expect—you can derive patterns out of most series of numbers. Take π again: 3.14 can be made into the equation $3 + 1 = 4$. It's more memorable that way.

Same for the natural logarithm ε, 2.71828. 2 into 7 yields a remainder of 1; 828 is nicely symmetrical, making the second three digits easy to recall.

John F. Kennedy was killed by an assassin's bullet on November 22, 1963. November 22, 1963, doesn't seem as if it contains a pattern, but 11/22/63 is more like it. Once you convert November 22 into 11/22, you'll never forget that part of the date. As for 63, well, 6 is twice three; the doubling pattern continues, only in reverse.

While I'm walking, sometimes for fun I keep my memory skills in shape by memorizing license plates. (I know, this may not *sound* like fun, but it sure beats focusing on how much farther it is till home while you're schlepping a heavy bag of groceries.) Recently, I spotted the following Washington, D.C., license plate: 43964. My mind went to work: Is there a pattern here? Yes: 4 is a perfect square; 3 squared is 9; and 64 is a perfect square. Those patterns may sound complicated, but they're not really. The brain *adores* patterns and continuity and once you've turned a seemingly random set of digits into a pattern or set of related patterns, you will remember it for as long as you want to.

The patterns don't have to be perfect to work; they don't have to be consistent throughout the number or numbers you're trying to learn. Once you force your mind's eye and brain to see the pattern, it will be ingrained in your memory. The very act of forcing yourself to create patterns where you never saw them before (and where most people don't see them) strengthens your memory of those digits.

Rhyme

Still another way to remember numbers is to turn them into rhyme. For example, if you have to remember that Route 28 is where the bridge you're going to have to travel over appears, create a rhyme: Twenty-eight, over the gate.

Practice

Use the skills you've developed so far to remember the following information:

Magainins, an extremely powerful antibiotic, were discovered in 1987.
The author of *The Student's Memory Book* was born on December 1.

The population of Huntsville, Alabama, in 1980 was 72,365.

Thomas Jefferson was the third President of the United States.

The human skeleton consists of 206 bones.

The first movie theater (called a nickelodeon) was built in Pittsburgh in 1905.

Montreal's population in 1980 was 1,080,546.

PART TWO

Applied Mnemonics

4

English Literature and "Rote" Memorization

There's practically no additional technique you need to learn to remember anything resembling English literature, such as Shakespeare, Chaucer, or poetry. You already have all the skills you'll need to remember plots, characters, interpretations, the life of the author, symbolism—whatever is on your "to do" list.

The most difficult problems you'll encounter when trying to accumulate information—because there's almost a limitless amount of detail you can acquire—are, first, determining what you want to remember and what isn't important, and second, organizing that material. The structure you give the information is absolutely essential to how well you remember it.

Two techniques you could use are to link information, using image association, or to employ the Top Ten system, described in Chapter 2. But instead let's use this chapter to develop two additional techniques that are also excellent tools for remembering large amounts of information.

The Room System

One of the limitations of the Top Ten system is that it is limited to lists of ten. For longer lists, you could create an extended Top Ten system and link the information you want to know to the images that represent the numbers 1 to 100, but doing that sounds tedious, and I won't break my promise that I will keep these memory systems fun. Fortunately, there's another way to remember large lists, the **Room system**, which is the oldest recorded mnemonic technique, used by the Greeks two thousand years ago. To remember things, the Greeks associated 1) what they wanted to know to 2) furniture (such as it was) in their homes. Because their furniture tended not to move around and because they could effortlessly remember where any piece of furniture was, the system was foolproof. When the Greeks recalled their furniture they always saw it in the same order around the room (left to right, most likely) and could be certain of reproducing that list or story in perfect order.

The Room system that you'll be using has an advantage over that of the Greeks—twentieth-century dwellers have more rooms and more furniture to serve as mnemonic loci than the Greeks did.

Your Room system will be personalized, because our houses have different rooms and different furniture. Although your system will look like no one else's, each Room system will be equally powerful.

Start by imagining the various rooms in your house. See them in the order in which you might walk through them when arriving home—first the living room, then the kitchen, then the dining room, then your bedroom, and so forth. The order should be natural. Figuratively walk through the rooms, noticing their spatial relationships.

Next, notice the furniture in each room. See the pieces as they are arranged. Pay attention only to those things you can see. If there's a painting behind a couch or a chair shunted away in a corner, ignore that. Also ignore windows and doors, unless they are particularly spectacular. Don't count furniture that is temporary or gets moved around.

Examine the rooms in a clockwise (left to right) direction, starting with the door or passage through which you enter. Always enter the room in the same way in your mind and always visualize in a clockwise direction. You should have no trouble establishing your Room system; in fact, you may discover that it is the easiest system in the book to learn.

Let's look at a hypothetical Room system. We'll include two rooms of a five-room house:

Room 1: The Living Room
(proceeding in a clockwise direction
from the house's entrance)

1. Couch
2. Love seat
3. Bookcase with books
4. TV
5. Stereo
6. Bar
7. Antique brass floor lamp
8. Lounge chair and ottoman

Room 2: The Kitchen

9. Sink
10. Dishwasher
11. Oven
12. Refrigerator

13. Butcher block table
14. Counter
15. Microwave oven
16. Telephone
17. Chalk board

To use the system, all you have to do is link what you want to remember to the items in your house. Because you always see these items in the same order, you will be able to remember lists in order.

(You can even use the Room system to remember lists that are tied to numbers, such as the periodic table of the elements, members of the Redskins football team, or exits on the highway.) Each item in your Room system also represents the same number—bar is 6 and the microwave is 15, for example. These household items and the numbers form an immutable relationship, so that if you want to remember the fifteenth item on a list you link that item to microwave oven. Because (once you've practiced the system) you can easily recall that microwave is also 15, remembering item 15 will pose no problem.

Macbeth

On to English literature. Let's take a look at Shakespeare's *Macbeth*. There are fourteen major characters in the play, so let's use the Room system to remember who they are. Keep in mind that while I'm using hypothetical rooms, you should use your own. Feel free to list rooms and what they contain before you start.

By the way, if you can, try to obtain artists' sketches of the characters in Macbeth. This will make it easier to remember them.

1. **Duncan** is King of Scotland; he is murdered by Macbeth.

Begin by linking Duncan to "couch," by seeing a king wearing a kilt sitting on the couch. What's he doing there?

He's eating a **Dunkin** doughnut; there's a box of Dunkin Donuts on his lap. As he's sitting on the couch he's knifed by another guy in a kilt who's wearing golden arches (stands for **Mac**,) on his shoulders and who leaped out of the **bath**.

2. **Macbeth** is a general in Duncan's army.

Visualize the Scottish general (Scots will always wear kilts in this mnemonic system) leaving the **bath**; the golden arches and stars on his shoulders signify rank as well as **Mac**. (Alternatively, you might want to visualize bathtubs under his eyes.) He's just killed someone—notice the bloody sword—and is resting on a love seat.

3. **Lady Macbeth** is ambitious and urges MacBeth to murder Duncan. Ultimately she goes mad.

Visualize a female version of Macbeth, also arising from the **bath**, but this time see the golden arches (**Mac**) in her hair. She takes a **book** from the **bookcase**—from your bookcase in your living room—and hits her husband with it. See her being led away to an insane asylum.

4. **Macduff** is the Scottish general who kills Macbeth.

Another Scottish general with golden arches for military braids; he's fat and looks **stuffed**. (You might also want to see him eating a stuffed Big Mac.) He bumps into your **TV**, which falls onto Macbeth and kills him.

5. **Banquo** is one of Duncan's generals and Macbeth's closest friend.

Another Scottish general. This one has a **bank** on top of his head. Visualize him leaving headquarters, Dunkin Donuts. He comes into your house, hugs Macbeth, and turns on the **stereo**. He and Macbeth relax to the music.

6. **Malcolm** is Duncan's oldest son. He flees to England after Duncan is killed.

Duncan's son—you can spot him by the **sunny** glow he has —is drinking **milk** from a **can**, though he's too old to be doing that. He realizes this chronological faux pas and gets a drink from the **bar**.

7. **Lennox** is one of Duncan's nobles.

Envision the nobleman also exiting Dunkin Donuts. He has a **line** through the X on his face. He's upset by the strange line and X on his face so he holds the **antique floor lamp** up to it to shed more light on these aberrations.

8. **Donalbain** is Duncan's youngest son. He flees to Ireland after Duncan is murdered.

Donalbain is actually **Donald** duck in disguise. Visualize the Donald Duck face on him and in place of his nose put a **bean,** so that you arrive at **Donald bean**. All he can do is **yawn,** which will remind you of young. He's tired and stretches out on the **lounge chair**.

9. **Ross** is Macduff's cousin and fulfills the role of a messenger in the play.

You can remember Ross by visualizing a Scotsman with a **rose** between his teeth. He brings **cows** (for "cousin") into Dunkin Donuts. When he returns to your house, he has to wash all that cow stuff off in your kitchen **sink**.

10. **Old Siward** is the Earl of Northumberland. He's on Macbeth's side.

Visualize an **old**-looking man with a **sewer** in place of his ears. Let the sewer plates resemble Old Siward's ears. Also in his ear is a **pearl;** the pearl is connected to a **thumb** with **land** around it. Siward is dirty, so he goes to clean himself in the **dishwasher.** (Apparently, he's not too familiar with how these things operate.)

11. **Young Siward** looks a lot like his father; the only difference is that Young Siward's eyes are like the **sun**. He goes to dry off in the **oven**.

12. **The Three Witches** prophesy Macbeth's ascension to the throne of Scotland as well as his demise.

Visualize three witches on top of a camel (remember, the image that represents 3). They are gazing into a crystal ball in which they see Macbeth. They put the crystal ball on top of the **refrigerator**. The ball is so heavy that the refrigerator sags in the middle.

13. **Seyton** is Macbeth's lieutenant.

Envision a soldier by Macbeth's side wearing **satin**. The soldier is eating a snack on *your* **butcher block table**.

14. **Porter** is the keeper of Macbeth's castle.

Fortunately, Porter bears semantic resemblance to his job; but you can also see a servant who looks like **pewter,** as if he's one of Macbeth's statues. Porter, among other things, cooks for Macbeth on top of the **counter**.

You'll notice that something else is going on here besides the mere linking of characters to fixed mnemonic points. In some of these instances we've actually created mini-stories to remember information about who killed whom and who was on which side. This comes naturally; in fact, it's more than natural to create sub-stories when trying to learn a play, novel, or poem, because that's what these things are—stories. Make your mnemonics into stories and you will have a far easier time remembering the information. Rely on the plot and relationships among the characters to guide your own sub-stories. Pretend you are a movie director and see the story evolve before your eyes.

Understanding characters' motivations helps tremendously. When you know *why* a character does something, that helps you remember what they do. So, as you're reading pay attention to what's going on. Question the characters and the author.

As you continue to read, question what's gone on previously. That will help you review the material.

"Rote" Memorization

You were wondering whether I would acknowledge that problem: What about when you have to memorize a passage verbatim? Are there any mnemonics that enable you to accomplish this onerous task?

Yes. But first two caveats. First, no one technique will work for all situations. Verbatim memorization is an integrated process involving several different memory systems in varying degrees. Second, mnemonics will not enable you to translate every word into an image that can be easily remembered. There's simply too much information—too many words—in most passages to learn. If, for example, you have to learn 300 lines in a play and each line contains 50 words, that's 15,000 words—creating 15,000 mnemonics would be tremendously time-consuming.

So what you do is use **sensible shortcuts.** (Simplifying life is a major theme of *The Student's Memory Book.)* Some of these shortcuts are obvious, but frequently dismissed: First, ignore articles ("the" and "a"), and forget about punctuation. Second, skip learning words that you find yourself already saying. Don't waste time and mental effort learning what you know.

Use the words you know—the ones that pop into your head automatically (often the ones that often *seem* to prevent you from learning the rest of the passage)—as a frame around which to build the rest of the quotation. **Link** what you do not know to what you already know. Let's look at the speech Macbeth gives after Macduff discovers King Duncan's assassination:

> Had I but died an hour before this chance,
> I had lived a blessed time; for from this instant,
> There's nothing serious in mortality:
> All is but toys: renown and grace is dead;

> The wine of life is drawn, and the mere lees
> Is left this vault to brag of.

I can't tell which words will stick in your cerebrum, because everyone has different natural abilities when it comes to memory. But let's say that in the first line you remember **I, died,** and **chance.** Perhaps you're having trouble with the beginning of the first line—you just can't seem to remember "Had . . . but." Applying mnemonics, your first task is to link **Had** to **I.** You can do this phonetically by visualizing a **hat** on an **eye.** Or you can think, "Macbeth didn't die. So the **died** in the line has to be made conditional." Once you look at the passage this way, remembering **Had I . . . died** will seem effortless. And you may discover that once you link **Had** and **I** together, the word **but** falls into place too. Next, connect **died** to **hour**—perhaps by seeing Duncan dying and falling onto an **hour**glass. (The mnemonic image you've created, an hourglass, will eventually give way to the words you want to remember.) The words **before, this,** and **chance** can be swallowed whole, because that's the way they make sense. Link **before this chance** to **hour** by creating an image for **before this chance:** see **chance** represented by dice; then link the image to **hour:** visualize the dice standing **before** the hourglass.

The place you are most likely to forget is between lines or sentences. It is between sentences that meaning changes, and this can pose a mental stumbling block. Alas, the tiny period (or a new line) seems to act as a major memory disrupter. Work on linking the last word of one sentence with the first word of the previous sentence. For example, lines 4 and 5: ". . . dead;/The wine . . ." You wouldn't want to link **dead** with **The,** so link it to **The wine:** Visualize a wine bottle resting in a coffin.

Essentially what you've done is to adapt the techniques you learned, substitution and the link, to rote memorization.

Still, even with the **sensible shortcuts**—ignoring articles, punctuation, and words you already know—using the link for rote memorization can be cumbersome.

As you discovered with the first line of this quotation, the more you memorize, the more additional words and phrases will fall into place. For example, you are struggling with the second line; you can remember **lived**, time, and **from this**, but can't seem to remember **blessed** and **instant**. When you link **blessed** to **time** (perhaps by seeing a priest blessing a clock) the word **instant** suddenly falls into place, because your mind sees a connection between **blessed** and **instant**.

But knowing more doesn't just pertain to individual words. The more you know about the target passage, the easier it will be to remember. Transliterate the quotation into your own words to get a better handle on what the speaker or author is trying to say. Ask yourself, what are the speaker's motivations? If you know that Macbeth is being a hypocrite, feigning grief for Duncan's murder, Macbeth's words become much easier to remember.

Another technique you can apply is to analyze the passage for interesting relationships among the words, phrases, and ideas. The first words of the first line of the Macbeth quotation begin, "Had I"; the second line starts with "I had." The first five lines have a reference to death or life: Line 1, **died**, line 2, **lived**, line 3, **mortality**, line 4, **dead**, line 5, **life** (again). There are even more patterns: In line 2, **instant** is a form of **time**.

As you memorize passages, you'll discover that particular phrases give you trouble. Focus your mnemonic talents on those problematic sections.

(There's yet another method, which has little to do with the techniques you've been learning, that can help you remember quotations. Tape yourself or a friend reciting the passage. Play the tape several times while you aren't doing anything strenuous.)*

---

* Thanks to Marta Vogel for telling me this trick.

In other words, do everything *except* rote memorization. Use sensible shortcuts and the link. Try to understand what the quotation is about and the speaker's or author's motivation. Finally look for phonetic and semantic patterns within the quotation.

The Rhyme List System

The Rhyme List system is identical in its application to the Top Ten system. The only difference between the two is that the former relies on the sounds of numbers, while the latter relies on the shapes of numbers. Some people are more comfortable with one than the other—use whichever you feel most drawn toward. It is, however, useful to know and practice both systems, because there will be occasions when you are required to memorize a couple of lists. Instead of piling all the information on the Top Ten system, you can spread what you need to know between the two.

Here is the system:

1 is bun
2 is shoe
3 is tree
4 is door
5 is hive
6 is sticks
7 is 7-Up
8 is gate
9 is vine
10 is hen

Let's apply this system to remembering the titles of the major poems of Walt Whitman's *Leaves of Grass*. They are

Inscriptions
Starting from Paumanok
Song of Myself
Children of Adam

Calamus
Drum-Taps
Out of the Cradle Endlessly Rocking
When Lilacs Last in the Dooryard Bloom'd
Crossing Brooklyn Ferry

To learn the first title, link "Inscriptions" to "bun" by seeing a poem inscribed on a hamburger bun.

To remember "Starting from Paumanok" you have to remember two pieces of information, **Starting** and **Paumanok**. First link "starting" to "shoe" by seeing a shoe poised at a **starting** line, but only a shoe. There's no one in the shoe, but there is a book of poetry in there. Link "Paumanok" to "shoe" by seeing a **palm** growing out of the shoe, too; there's a ham**mock** in the palm tree.

The next poem is "Song of Myself." See a tree singing. It's holding up a mirror and singing to itself.

For "Children of Adam," first link "Children" in a meaningful way to "door" by visualizing plenty of children trying to rush through a door at the same time. Next link "children" to "Adam" by seeing the children held back by **a dam**.

The fifth poem is "Calamus," which can easily be linked to hive. After you're stung by bees that come from the hive, what you naturally do is put **Calamine** lotion on. When using mimicry to create a mnemonic be sure to pay extra attention to detail. Just hearing a phonetic connection is never enough —it is your mind's eye that's powerful.

"Drum-Taps" is the sixth poem in *Leaves of Grass*. Connect that to sticks by seeing someone drumming on **tacks** with sticks.

The seventh poem is "Out of the Cradle Endlessly Rocking," which presents a little more difficulty than "Drum-Taps": There are several words that we have to remember. First, break the poem's title into meaningful components. They are 1) Out, 2) Cradle, and 3) Endlessly Rocking. It's best to start with the most substantive part of the title, "Cra-

dle." (You might be inclined to create a mnemonic in the
order that the words appear. That's okay, of course, but it's
usually easier to create a mnemonic starting with the most
concrete word. This will make a stronger cue. It only becomes important to create your mnemonic in word order
when you're liable not to know the order of words intuitively.
In this case there's only one word order that makes sense, so
the conscious, thinking part of your brain will automatically
take care of word order.) Okay—Cradle to 7-Up is easy
enough. See a cradle filled with full 7-Up bottles. (Make sure
you see them full; detail contributes to your ability to remember the image.) Next connect "Endlessly Rocking" to "Cradle" by seeing it rocking and rocking and rocking on its end.
Finally, connect "Endlessly Rocking" to "Out" by visualizing someone taking the 7-Up bottles **out** of the cradle, much
to the consternation of the baby who's in there. Notice that if
we had created an image for "Out" before we made linked
"Cradle" and 7-Up, we probably would have had a different,
and weaker, image for "Out."

"When Lilacs Last in the Dooryard Bloom'd" is the eighth
poem. Same problem as above and same solution—break it
into its component parts. Connect "Lilacs" to gate, the mnemonic for 8, by seeing a gate smothered in lilacs. (If you
don't know what a lilac looks like you could substitute and
see **lying ax**, but you're much better off taking a few minutes
to track down a picture of a lilac and using that image.) Link
"Last" to "Lilacs" by seeing them **last** through the winter.
There's snow on the ground, of course. Next link "Dooryard" to "Last" by seeing a snow-covered door in the yard,
leaning against the gate. The lilacs are even lasting while
there's a door leaning against them! "Bloom'd" is the last
word: you could see the lilacs blooming, or you could see
them **booming**, whichever works better for you.

The final Whitman poem is "Crossing Brooklyn Ferry."
See a **cross** covered in a vine. Can you envision the vine and

cross on the Brooklyn Bridge? The cross falls off the bridge (probably because of a stiff breeze) and into the river, where it lands on a **ferry** boat that (for mnemonic reinforcement) is filled with fairies.

5

The Histories

History is fascinating—all those facts are like a gigantic trivia game. But history is a burdensome thing to master: All those facts to learn! Once you read this chapter "all those facts" will no longer be a problem—information will stick to your mind like a wine stain on a white rug. The techniques presented in this chapter apply equally well to all areas of history including, American history, history of art, Russian history, intellectual history, and the history of science.

Why History Is So Hard to Remember

There are usually five elements that students of history have to be concerned about memorizing: 1) Remembering individuals (otherwise known as historical figures), 2) remembering places (frequently called countries, city-states, and battle locations), 3) learning about inventions (sometimes called magic or high-tech, depending on the era), 4) being aware of what happened, which incorporates the "why" and "what" of an event, and 5) memorizing the date, a bit of detail that lets you know in what order things happened. What makes history so difficult a subject to master is that to make sense of it (and do things like pass an exam or write a paper) you have to know all of these elements. It does no good, for example, to know that the Civil War was a war between the North and South if you can't place the century. It's also helpful, for example, if you're studying communications, to know who invented the telephone and the radio and in what countries these inventors lived.

History, because it is so all-encompassing, requires that you use just about every mnemonic technique you know. The cue, image association, and surprise seeing are paramount, but you'll discover that mimicry is vital, because names of leaders, scientists, and places are essential to learning history.

History Made Easy

But there's a trick to learning history, too: Many historical events repeat themselves (some say that history doesn't repeat itself, it's just historians who repeat each other). War, famine, the invention of . . . , and being crowned are examples—they have occurred hundreds of time throughout recorded history. To make learning history easier, create a mnemonic for each of these common events and use that mnemonic each time the particular event occurs. For example, victorious in battle becomes a victor, beaming a smile, standing on top of the vanquished, who is lying on the ground; friendship, treaty, or normalizing relations is shaking hands; independence (some countries have it and some don't) is raising a flag with fireworks sparkling.

Because many events that you will want to convert into

mnemonics are action scenes, they will lend themselves easily to mnemonic images. Just think in terms of pictures when you try to memorize history. This is true when working with wars, inventions, natural disasters—and people! If what you are memorizing involves an actual person, try to find a picture of that individual. I call this the comic-book approach, and it works. Look at the photograph or drawing as you create a mnemonic for the person's name. Link the mnemonic to that picture. Most students never look at pictures when they try to learn historical material. But actually seeing an image of what you want to memorize will automatically make memorizing the information two or three times easier. These history-specific mnemonics are described in the chronology that follows.

A Historical Time Frame

This chronology will also give you a frame of reference for world history. You'll know some of the most important whos and whats; you'll know that the *Canterbury Tales* were written after Genghis Khan's rule. In addition to being a whiz at Trivial Pursuit and Jeopardy, you'll have world history at your fingertips. Because events are intertwined, this chapter will give you a better sense of how events can affect each other across the centuries. The events described in this chapter are navigating maps that put everything else into perspective.

Not every important historical event is included in this chronology; that would take an entire book. However, a representative number of important events from a variety of histories are presented here. You'll learn about key events in the history of religion, art history, American history, ancient history, the history of science, and literature.

You can learn the information in this entire chapter if you want—that's your best option because then you'll have a chronology of twenty-five hundred years of human history at your fingertips. Or you can simply learn selected bits, if you're pressed for time.

Remembering Dates

You don't always have to remember the full date—month, day and year—to learn it. Usually, when you are focusing on dates that are entirely within one century, you can ignore the century and just pay attention to the decade and the year. In other words, you may forget the first digit out of the four digits that make up a year. It makes sense to minimize the amount of work you have to do. For example, if you are learning the chronology of the Civil War, don't bother to make a mnemonic for 18xx, just focus on the last two digits. And if you already know that the Civil War took place entirely during the 1860s, then only the last digit is significant. Another example: when you're examining Elizabethan England, just the last three or two digits will suffice; your common sense won't confuse 1572 with 572. That makes your task easier and swifter. If you only have one (or two) digits to memorize, instead of the four that normally constitute a year, you will have more time to learn other details.

Months

Depending on the depth of detail you want to acquire, you may or may not need to know what month something occurred in. In case you do, here's a mnemonic chart for remembering months.

January	A **janitor** eating a **berry**
February	**Feet brewing**
March	**Marching**
April	**A veil**
May	May flowers—that is, plenty of bright, colorful flowers
June	June bride—a crowd of brides
July	**A jewel**

August	**A gust** of wind
September	**Swept under**
October	**Octopus** (or a pumpkin)
November	A turkey
December	Christmas tree

Want to remember December 8, 1987, the year the United States and Soviet Union signed the Intermediate Nuclear Force Treaty? Connect a hive to a Christmas tree by attaching it to a branch like an ornament.* (See the bees buzzing.) Next link the scene to 7 (you obviously know the decade) by placing a key in the hive. The key opens the hive, and there are nuclear missiles locked inside. The President is autographing the missiles. (You can add more information to this mnemonic if you want.)

Historical Time Line

(Consult the chapter on geography for mnemonics pertaining to specific countries.)

And now, without further suspense, here are some of the highlights of world history:

Alexander the Great invaded India in 327 B.C.
Create an image of Alexander the Great: A well-shaven man (Alexander was reputed to have been the first Greek person to shave), dressed in Greek clothing, on a horse, marching into a bottle of **India** ink, or marching into the Taj Majal, the symbol for India. He is being followed by a **monk**.

Liu Pang assumed the role of emperor of China in 202 B.C.
Picture Liu Pang, a man in emperor-style clothing **leaping** over the Great Wall of China. He's able to accomplish that feat because he takes his **niacin** tablet.

---

* Chapter 3, Numbers, teaches a phonetic system for learning numbers. That system is a prerequisite for this chapter.

The Roman ruler Julius Ceasar was murdered in 44 B.C.

Picture a Roman emperor (your stereotyped image) with a **caesar** salad on top of his head instead of a crown. He is being beaten to death with a **rare** steak.

The Jewish uprising against the Romans under Bar Kokhba began in A.D. *132.*

Visualize people carrying shields with Stars of David on them in a **bar**. They get mad because the bar tries to run away. They try to **catch** the bar. They run outside into the Roman Coliseum, where they are captured. The Romans are **taming** them.

Diophantus, in Alexandria, produced the first book about algebra in about the year 250. (Now you know where to place the blame.)

A **dio**de-covered **fan** is being waved by an erudite-looking person with a slide rule, calculator, and lots of pens in his pocket. Obviously a mathematician. He's writing equations in a book—every possible millimeter of the book and its cover is covered with equations. But he's becoming frustrated with these algebraic equations, as anybody would, and is hammering **nails** into the book.

The Huns withdrew from Europe in approximately 470. (Attila died in 453.)

Imagine a map of Europe (or the Concorde jet, the symbol for Europe) coated with **hon**ey. Just smeared with the stuff. Somebody has turned the map over on its side and is trying to get the honey off (a kind of withdrawal). It's not an easy task, so that **rakes** have to be used to remove the honey. Alternatively, you could envision soldiers covered with honey—the Huns—standing on a map of Europe or inside the Concorde: they have to be taken off with rakes.

King Arthur of the Britons was killed in the Battle of Camlan in 537.

Art, a painting, with **fur** around the frame (or a painting

with fur in place of paint); the painting (anthropomorphized)
is wearing a crown and royal robes. (Still another alternative:
If you can create your own image for King Arthur, based on
a movie or your imagination, that would work best of all).
The painting is situated in the middle of a battlefield; strewn
across the **land** are **cameras**. A **lime** is thrown at the painting
and the lime lands with a whack.

Mohammed, the founder of Islam, is born in A.D. *570.*
Mowing with a **hammer** around a Mosque; the Mosque is
also surrounded by **lakes**.

Charlemagne embarked on the subjugation of Saxony in
772.
A man with a **scarlet mane** (or a **champagne** bottle in the
form of a man) standing on top of a **saxophone** and wrapping
that saxophone in a **cocoon**.

The collection of tales in A Thousand and One Nights *be-*
gun in 900.
Visualize 1001 nights—darkness after darkness after darkness. The only thing to do during those nights is listen to
stories (tales) and eat **pizzas**.

The first Viking colonies were established in Greenland in
982.
People **biking** to a land that is entirely **green** (they are
wearing Viking-style helmets) and look like **buffoons**.

The epic poem Beowulf *was written down in the year 1000.*
A **bay** with **wolfs** in it; the wolfs are singing poems. The
wolfs **toss saws**.

The Norman invasion of England occurred in 1066.
A **normal man** breaking through the doors that open onto
England. He stubs his **toes** and as a result has to do the **cha-
cha** instead of walking.

The Chinese first used explosives in war in 1161.
Picture the Great Wall of China being blown up by primitive explosives—fireworks kind of explosives. A **tot** takes a **shot** at the fallen wall.

Genghis Khan became prince of the Mongols in 1206.
Envision Genghis Khan not as an individual but as a **gang** of people in one body—that body resembles King **Kong**. The Khan is dressed in the now familiar symbol for a king, prince, or queen—a crown and royal robes. He is addressing his people, all of whom are wearing **monocles**. They are also dressed for **tennis** and are shouting "**Wish**" while they listen.

King John signed the Magna Carta in 1215.
A **john** with a crown on top; inside this toilet is a document. Someone **carts** the paper away and reads it with a **mag**nifying glass. They then put the Magna Carta in a **tent** to dry and to protect it from the hail.

(There's a somewhat popular and certainly effective mnemonic used by some students that can be helpful in remembering this date: "The Magna Carta was signed right after lunch, at 12:15 P.M.)†

Marco Polo started his journey to China in 1271.
A man with a strange **mark**, the design of the Great Wall of China, on his head, playing **polo** in front of the Wall. He's wearing a **tunic** (or drinking a **tonic**). On top of the tunic is a **hat**.

The Crusades ended in 1291.
Horsemen carrying crosses returning from the Middle East (they have sand in their clothes); their swords are bloodied and they are carrying **tin** cups filled with **pine** cones.

The Hundred Years' War began in 1337.
Because the war is going on so long, women and children are continually mopping their tears with **tissues**. Alterna-

† My thanks to Jill Bogard for telling me this.

tively, you might envision soldiers using tissues instead of white flags to indicate surrender; if you do, actually see them take the tissues from a Kleenex box. The dead soldiers are whisked away into a tomb, still others get stuck in muck, can't move, and are killed.

The bubonic plague (black death) began in China in 1332 and from there spread to Europe. (A third of Europe, 75 million people, died between 1347 and 1351.)

Imagine sickly rats with fleas on them—a scene out of a horror movie—biting and walking among people, who are dying. See the people covered with a black shroud or shadow as they become sick. The dead are carried away into a tomb, the others moan.

Chaucer wrote The Book of the Duchess in 1369.

A man writing with chalk in a book that has lots of pictures of ducks in it. Fortunately the ducks are tame, but that's only because they are on their way to shop.

The Great Schism began in 1378 (and lasted until 1417) after the death of Pope Gregory XI. (Two Popes were elected, Urban VI in Rome and Clement VII in Avignon.)

Visualize two popes standing on opposite sides of a canyon, a great divide. They are choosing members of their team from amongst the various bishops and priests standing in the canyon. They write down the names of their team members on their cuffs.

Joan of Arc led the French armies against England in 1429.

A pair of jeans with an arch in them (you're not likely to think "Jean" of Arc); but if you prefer, envision a joker. This woman (who can also look like the singer Joan Jett or the actress Joan Crawford, if you prefer) is leading all these men with berets and carrying swords. Joan of Arc is captured: There's a tear in her eye; she takes a nap.

The cast-iron gun the "Mad Marjorie" is introduced into warfare in 1430.

Use your imagination to picture a very primitive gun—big, bulky, doesn't fire all that well; in fact, it fires not lead bullets, but **tar**. It is first used to shoot at **moose**.

The Turks captured Constantinople and killed Emperor Constantine XI in 1453, ending the Byzantine (Eastern Roman) Empire.

Soldiers dressed in turkey costumes capturing **cantaloupes** (with legs, arms, etc.—cantaloupe animals. They put the cantaloupe animals in a **cone**-shaped **stein** being held by a **tot**. The cantaloupe animals are put on **trial**, whereupon they are then beaten with a **ham**.

Gutenberg printed with movable type for the first time in 1453; he prints the Mainz Bible.

A **good burger** is accidentally run through an old-style printing press; because this happens in the fifteenth century when magic is still possible (and because it's the first press and not everything works properly), the burger is transformed into a Bible. Well, it's not actually a Bible, but a book containing a **maze**. Anyway, since it's a primitive operation, the paper goes directly from the **tree** to the **loom**.

In 1492 Leonardo da Vinci drew his flying machine.

In some cases it's not necessary to create a picture out of somebody's name where that name already lends itself to an image. Almost everyone has seen pictures of Leonardo da Vinci; most of us have even seen sketches of Leonardo with his flying machine. So melt that picture into your mind. Take five seconds to envision it. Then to recall that this happened in 1492, see a **tire** on the flying machine that's attached to a **bone** which is being used as an axle.

Also in 1492, Christopher Columbus sailed from Spain to the New World.

There's no better way to remember this fact than through

the old rhyme, "In fourteen hundred ninety-two, Columbus
sailed the ocean blue."

Thomas Cromwell was executed in 1540.

Let **thumb** flicking **crumbs** into a **well** represent Thomas
Cromwell. See the thumb cut off from the hand—executed,
as it were—and subsequently there are **tailors** who try to fit
the thumb with clothes for burial.

Shakespeare wrote Romeo and Juliet *in 1594.*

If you can't conjure an image of William Shakespeare, then
envision a man trying to write with a spear instead of a pen; it
doesn't work of course, so he's **shaking** the **spear**. He's shaking the spear at the two lovers, one of whom is drinking **rum**,
the other is wearing lots of **jewels**. The man gives the woman
a **tulip** which vanishes into air.

*Two years later, in 1593, Galileo invented a simple open-air
thermometer.*

A man encased in a **galaxy** having his temperature taken
with a crude **thermometer** (boy does it hurt!). He's covered
with a **towel** that's catching blood pouring off him; the blood
is spilling onto a **poem** he was reading.

*Rembrandt painted the "Portrait of an Eighty-three-year-
old Woman" in 1636.*

Rembrandt sitting on a **rim** of a **branch** painting an elderly
woman with **foam** on her. The woman is sitting on another
branch, close enough so Rembrandt can just **touch** her, but
not by **much**.

*The British Parliament passed the Stamp Act taxing Ameri-
can colonies, which created an uproar in the Virginia Assembly and elsewhere in 1765. Congress convened in New York
and the nine colonies drew up a declaration of rights and
liberties. (The Stamp Act was repealed in 1766.)*

There is a wealth of information here. As with other infor-
mation-dense matter, it's best to separate the details into

components. First, create a picture involving the British Parliament passing the Stamp Act with a notion that the Stamp Act has something to do with taxes. If you can conjure a clear image of the British Parliament in your mind, terrific; if not create a reasonably realistic picture of what you *think* it should look like. The simplest way to do this is to start with the U.S. Congress and change it into something British by adding English muffins to the scene, or by making the Parliamentarians wear those silly wigs. They vote, and as a result of their vote they pass around stamps. The stamps are posted to America, and the recipients have a horrified look on their faces because the price of the new stamps is incredibly high. (Alternatively, you can put tacks through the stamps.) People are so mad that in one colony (New York) they are throwing around **new corks**; in another (Virginia) **virgins** are being sacrificed.

If you want to know that there were nine colonies at the time, make a picture of the colonists enclosed in a hoop.

The colonists are writing and drawing at the same time: Their pictures include bells, for liberty, and scales, for justice. See the bells and scales as boldly, as brilliantly, as you can.

Should you want to know that the Stamp Act was repealed in 1766, take stamps and put them on a piece of **teak**, **chew** them, and hit them with a **shoe**.

The American Revolution began in 1775 with Paul Revere's ride from Boston to Lexington. (The Declaration of Independence was issued in 1776, but presumably nobody needs a mnemonic to remember that.)

Lots of Uncle Sams dressed in uniform and carrying guns are marching on the battlefield. They are being led by a man on horseback shouting, "The Redcoats are coming! The Redcoats are coming!" He has a big **paw** cupped in front of his mouth. **Paw** Revere has just left Boston (a town whose streets are paved with beans) and is riding to **Lexington** (Avenue—if you can visualize New York City), a **leg**-filled town. He

pauses to bow and removes his hat, takes a sip of Coke, then
proceeds to ride up a steep hill.

Edward Jenner introduced smallpox vaccination in 1796.

Sometimes you don't need to remember all the information
contained in a particular text. For example, you may decide
that *who* created the smallpox vaccine isn't relevant, and just
focus on learning that the vaccine was invented in 1796. And
even if you do decide to remember that Jenner was the inven-
tor, knowing that his first name is Edward may not be important. Select the information you want to know: Decide what's
important and focus on that.

So let's focus on the smallpox vaccine and not Edward
Jenner. (Whose name you probably will remember, as it was
mentioned several times in the previous and current para-
graphs.)

The smallpox vaccine can be visualized in one of several
ways. You can imagine hundreds of children with that horrible disease over them: vaccinations cure them miraculously.
Or you can see children—again, hundreds is better than one
—with **small picks** on the surface of their skin, and a vaccination removes them. (Never mind that vaccines are designed
to prevent disease and not cure it; the images we are creating
will work for what we want to remember.) Finally, you could
see a man being examined in a doctor's office. His problems is
that he has cows (cowpox and smallpox)—little cows sprout-
ing from his skin, borrowed from a Gary Larson cartoon.

When the doctor removes the offending scars, small picks
or cows, they hoot. He places them in a **cube**, whereupon
they turn to **ash**.

Napoleon was defeated in Moscow in 1812.

Napoleon is an easy enough character to visualize: A
short, squat man in uniform with his hand stuck in his jacket.
(The reason for that only *your imagination* knows; it's because he's hiding a napoleon pastry there.) See him and his
army being routed by soldiers riding **masked cows**. As they

retreat, Napoleon and his soldiers eat toffee they pull out of a tin.

The Monroe doctrine was issued in 1823; it prohibited European nations from colonizing the Americas.

For Monroe, envision a President wearing a **monocle** who is rowing off the coast of South America. The monocled President is leaving behind paper—documents—which are being set up as barriers around the continent. Europeans—Englishmen with their muffins, the French with their wineglasses, the Germans driving their (old-fashioned) Mercedes—are trying to penetrate the barrier, but can't. The Europeans are shot at: see a bullet piercing a hat. The Europeans retreat in a **van** to home.

The First Opium war between Britain and China began in 1839.

For opium, envision the poppy fields from *The Wizard of Oz,* or opium being smoked through a pipe. Picture British and Chinese soldiers fighting in an opium field—they are becoming high. The field is surrounded by a gate, which in turn is surrounded by **foam**, which is surrounded by a hoop.

Henry David Thoreau wrote "Walden" in 1854.

If you can successfully picture Thoreau sitting by Walden Pond, terrific. If not, picture this writer **throwing** books into a pond that is **walled in.** A goat fell into the lake to rescue the books (goats eat paper, after all); the goat realizes it can't swim and will have to row.

On April 12, 1861, the Civil War began as the Confederates took Fort Sumter, in Charleston.

You'll probably notice something different about this date: A month and a day are included. (And you thought remembering just the year was quite a feat—wait until you're able to remember the day of the month, too.)

Let's work with the date first in this case: Connect **a veil** (the symbol for April) to **town** (or Tina, if you know somebody by that name) by having a veil over a whole town. Make this into a concrete image.

Now for the rest of the date, 1861. See toffee throughout the town's streets. There's a war going on, so the toffee is being shot. See the soldiers shooting the toffee.

You know it's the Civil War because there are **onions** (Union) battling **confetti** (Confederate).

The confetti-throwing soldiers are throwing confetti because they have just captured a fort with **some tar** around it.

Because of the battle the city has become a **char**red town.

And that's all you need to do to learn when and where the Civil War began.

President Abraham Lincoln's Emancipation Proclamation took effect January 1, 1863.

Everybody should be able to conjure an image of Abraham Lincoln; if you can't, take out a five-dollar bill and stare at the drawing. Imagine Lincoln walking to a place where slaves are held—he is speaking, and setting them free. (This image is a crude abstraction of what happened as a consequence of the Emancipation Proclamation, but it is enough for our purposes.)

Now let's link that to 1/1/1863. Envision a janitor eating a berry and he's picking the berries out of a hat. The hat is covered with toffee which is covered with ash which is, in turn, attached to a ham. A ridiculous image, perhaps; but if you make it strong enough, you will remember it forever.

In 1880 Thomas Edison received a patent for the electric light.

A **tom**-tom floating in the eddies. Although the **sun** is shining brightly, it's possible to see the light from bulbs on top of the tom-tom. As someone who's wearing **patent** leather shoes plays the tom-toms, the lights flash in synchronization with the music. Just then another person pulls out of a hat several **fifes** and passes them around, and everyone begins to play music. As the music is played, the light bulbs flash even more.

Henry Ford built his first car in 1892.

A **hungry fork** being used to construct a car—not doing well, because the fork is eating car parts. (You probably already know that Henry Ford built the first assembly-line American automobile; if so, just focus on linking a car—a primitive, first car—to the date. As always, minimize the amount of information you need to learn.) The car gets stuck in **toffee**, then a **pin** punctures its tire.

The Boxer uprisings in China against the Europeans occurred in 1900.

Visualize **boxes** (or Chinese soldiers just in **boxer** shorts) fighting against Europeans in front of the Great Wall of China. (It's always good to place any scene that involves China in front of the Great Wall, the easiest mnemonic for China.) Imagine the French with wineglasses, the English with their muffins, the Germans with their VWs. The Chinese have a new weapon—a **top** they can use with devastating consequences. Then the Chinese come after the Europeans with **saws**.

The Russo-Japanese war began in 1904.

Russians—noticeable because of their furry hats—fighting Japanese—noticeable because they carry transistor radios. The battle is going on inside a **tub**; the water in the tub has become **sour**.

World War I began on July 28, 1914, with the assassination in Sarajevo of Archduke Franz Ferdinand, heir to the Austrian throne, and his wife.

First, decide what of this information you want to remember. In our case, we will strive to retain everything. (Generally—although an exam question may not ask about a particular fact, such as *where* Ferdinand was killed—the more detail you demonstrate, the more impressed the professor will be and the greater the chances of your receiving the benefit of his doubt.)

Because there are eight discrete bits of information contained in that sentence, we're going to construct a kind of mnemonic Rube Goldberg apparatus. First let's start with WWI because any question is likely to ask, "When did the First World War begin?" rather than "What happened when Archduke Ferdinand was assassinated?" *It's always best to remember the information in order of importance.* It's easy enough to create a memorable image for World War I: Picture a globe; rising from the globe's surface are armies and soldiers, biplanes, poison gas—all sorts of images to represent a world conflagration.

So now when you see or hear a question referring to World War I, the picture of a globe covered with machines of war will pop into mind.

Now connect that image with the date, July 28, 1914. See the soldiers throwing jewels (symbol for July) at one another; or perhaps they are thwarting attacks with jewel-studded shields. Link jewel to 28, or a word with the n-f sound, such as knife. Then link "knife" to the year. Notice that you don't have to find a mnemonic for the 19xx part of 1914. Everybody knows what century World War I began. This is true for most events in the twentieth century: we generally don't need to learn what the first two digits are. So translate 14 into an image and link it to knife: perhaps the knives are turning into tar, or into a tear.

Now for the cast of characters. First, Archduke Franz Ferdinand, heir to the Austrian throne. He's the one whose death was the catalyst for this whole war.

To remember that Ferdinand is an archduke, tuck the image of **duck**ing under an **arch** in mind as you play with his name. Ferdinand can be remembered by imagining a **furry band**age. The man who's wearing this furry Band-Aid is **frowning** because he has to duck under an arch. As he ducks under the arch, he becomes a proverbial sitting duck and is

shot. Dead. And so is his wife, who has even more trouble
than Franz in ducking under the arch. They fall on the
ground and end up with sandy elbows—really picture the
sandy elbows.

All that's left is to connect Archduke Ferdinand with
World War I, and that's easy. Just see soldiers start shooting
each other after the Archduke is shot: the fighting spreads
around the world.

When dealing with dates, from this point on we're only
going to bother with the last two digits of the century. Most
events that took place in the twentieth century are unmis-
takenly twentieth century—that is, they are not likely to be
confused with other centuries.

*In 1916 Albert Einstein postulated his general theory of rel-
ativity.*

Picture an **eye** in a beer **stein** (you already know Einstein's
first name, so there's no sense in developing a mnemonic for
it). Link that with general theory of relativity, or theory of
relativity for short, or simply relativity—which is certainly
enough to invoke the rest of that phrase. You can see **relatives** of the eye around the stein, or see the eye moving within
the stein in a **relativistic** way. Or if you know that one of
Einstein's most important predictions, that space is curved
and its greatest curvature occurs around objects with large
mass, and that this theory was tested by observing a distant
star's light bend around the sun during a solar eclipse—then
you could see another eye eclipsing the first eye.

As for 1916. We've agreed to skip the 19xx portion, because the date is obviously *not* 1816. Connect the eye to **dish**
by putting an eye on one. (See Chapter 3, Numbers, for the
complete list of standard mnemonics.)

*The 19th Amendment to the Constitution, granting women
the right to vote, was ratified in 1920.*

Envision women being prevented by men from entering

voting booths. Suddenly out of the corner of the room a magician is revealed who turns these men into hot **ash**, thereby allowing the women to vote. The magician is carrying a large —larger than life—document, the Constitution; he scoops up the hot **ash** and rubs it onto the Constitution, whereupon the ash turns into words, the 19th Amendment. He then carefully places the Constitution in a **noose**.

The Russian Revolution—the overthrow of the czars—happened in 1917.
Lots of **czars**—a kind of celebration—being thrown out the windows of St. Basil's Cathedral (or some other building that conjures Russia in your mind). Next, each has his **hat** thrown out, which lands on an **oak**.

On July 16, 1945, the first atomic bomb was exploded near Alamogordo, New Mexico.
An atomic bomb exploding is not too difficult to envision; to enhance the notion that this was the first detonation, see people standing around watching the explosion wearing 3-D glasses, the kind that people wear to view a 3-D movie. See lots of **armadillos** blown into the atmosphere by the explosion. The explosion also creates a **mixed Coke** (New Mexico).
Connect this image with the date, July 16, 1945: Deep inside the mushroom cloud is a **jewel** with an **oat** growing out of it, with **ash** on that oat. The whole apparatus is sliding along a **rail**.

The Potsdam treaty was signed in 1945.
There are **pots** falling over a **dam**. See **tub** being caught by a **reel** as it spills over the side of the dam.

On July 21, 1969, Neil Armstrong became the first human to walk on the moon.
An astronaut, kneeling and walking on his arms—because they are **strong**—on the surface of the moon. People around

are applauding, naturally because he's the first from earth to do such a thing. They give him a jewel, but the jewel gets stolen by a lunar gnat, which then flies away to its ship.

And the rest, so to speak, is history.

6

Languages

Foreign languages can be enjoyable, but language is one subject where getting there can be no fun at all. Learning thousands of foreign words, comprehending and memorizing new grammar, figuring out how to use idioms, knowing what adjective ending goes with what noun ending, and getting verb tense right and pronunciation perfect are arduous tasks.

Learning languages can be divided into components: 1) understanding the new grammar, 2) practicing the language, and 3) memorizing. Of these, memorization is the biggest stumbling block: all those words, idioms, and exceptions make the task appear overwhelming. While foreign grammar is also difficult, part of its difficulty revolves around having a weak vocabulary; understanding grammar and being able to use it is highly dependent on having the right words at your disposal—in other words, the vocabulary.

There are three techniques you'll be using to learn foreign words: the mimicry, the link, and the cue. You'll be transforming abstract-sounding nonsense sounds into concrete images through mimicry, and then linking these images to the word you want to remember. However, it won't always be necessary to mimic the word because many foreign language words have a phonetic relationship to English. Look out for these. The Spanish words *historia* (history), *nuevo* (new), and *diccionario* (dictionary) are three examples.

The steps involved in creating a mnemonic for a foreign vocabulary word are straightforward. First, substitute an English word or phrase for the word you want to learn. Then create an image that corresponds to that word. Try to make the image bear a semantic relationship to the word's meaning. This won't always be possible, but it's worth the effort because you will have a double link between the mnemonic and the foreign word. For example, the french word for mushroom is *champignon*. It sounds like "shompinon," which can be substituted for **chomping on**. Imagine a mushroom chomping on a steak and you'll remember that mushroom is *champignon*.

When you learn foreign vocabulary this way, you automatically create two cues. The first is the mimicked sound, which lets you recall the word in one direction: from the foreign language to English. For example, when you hear "shompinon," your mind will make the connection between it and **chomping on**, and then you will see the mushroom. The second cue, the image you've created, enables you to recall the foreign word when someone asks you for the English translation for that word. For example, when you think mushroom, you see a mushroom, and the image of a **mushroom chomping** comes into your mind's eye.

The one limitation mimicry has is that when reading foreign languages, you have to **hear** the word in order for your mind to conjure the mnemonic. Mimicry works by image and sound; if you just read the word printed on a page, chances are that you won't be able to recall it's mnemonic or meaning. Using tapes in conjunction with mnemonics is helpful.

The more you use mnemonics the less you will have to rely on them. Mnemonics are only a temporary measure, to bridge the time between when you encounter a foreign language word and when you eventually *know* it.

Some Foreign Language Examples
(Consult your language text for the precise pronunciation.)

French

Word	*poulet*
Pronunciation	poolay
Meaning	chicken
Mimic	pulling the leg of a chicken
Word	*canard*
Pronunciation	kanard
Meaning	duck
Mimic	how hard it is to get a duck into a can
Word	*jambon*
Pronunciation	jam bone
Meaning	ham
Mimic	jamming a bone into the face of a pig

Italian

Word	*buon*
Pronunciation	bwon
Meaning	good
Mimic	be on good behavior
Word	*serà*
Pronunciation	sarah
Meaning	night (as in good night)
Mimic	say, rough night

Word	*ciao*
Pronunciation	chow
Meaning	see ya
Mimic	have to go eat chow, now

Word	*bene*
Pronunciation	bainay
Meaning	fine
Mimic	Benny Goodman, a fine musician

Word	*freddo*
Pronunciation	fraydoa
Meaning	cold
Mimic	frozen over

Word	*chiuso*
Pronunciation	keeoosoa
Meaning	shut
Mimic	key use (to open)

Word	*vecchio*
Pronunciation	vehkeeoa
Meaning	old
Mimic	vacuum over (because it's old)

Word	*adesso*
Pronunciation	ahdehso
Meaning	now
Mimic	address those (now!)

Word	*cugino*
Pronunciation	koojeeno
Meaning	cousin
Mimic	cool jeans that your cousin is wearing

Word	*tempo*
Pronunciation	tehmpo
Meaning	time
Mimic	a clock's ticking is a tempo

Russian

Languages that use a foreign alphabet, such as Russian, are no more difficult to learn than Romance languages. The trick is to focus on the sounds of the words, not their spelling. Once you learn foreign vocabulary phonetically, you will have little trouble recognizing written words. Learning foreign vocabulary this way is natural—it's the way children learn language: first the words as they sound, then as they are written. Approaching a foreign language that uses a foreign alphabet phonetically will strengthen your speaking ability in that language.

English	Russian Transliteration and Pronunciation	Mimic
Fool	Durak doo-rock	Somebody hitting a **rock** against their head. That's very foolish.
Place or spot	Mesto Me-yes-ta	See your apartment **messed up**
When	Kogda cog-da	When can you use the rest room? When the **cog** (somebody in your office) is done with it.
Good	Horosho harra-sho	The opposite of good? **Horror show!**
Good morning	Dobroye utro dough-bray ootra	It's 6 A.M. There's that damn **doberman hooting** again.

Japanese

Sometimes you need to learn a phrase—because it's an idiom or because you use that phrase frequently—rather than an individual word. Mnemonics works as well for phrases as it does for single words.

Creating mnemonics for phrases is more complicated than it is for words; however, as with most memory techniques, the more you practice, the better you will become. As always, make sure that you have a clear picture of the mimic you've created, and, if possible, relate that image to the meaning of the original phrase. Remember, the mimicry does not have to sound one hundred percent like the original phrase, just close enough for you to remember it.

How do you do?

JEE-meh-mahsh-teh, DOH-zoh yoh ROH-shee-koo

Gee, me mashed the dough. Do you roll sheets? Oo!

Add a semantic component to the mimic. See two bakers being introduced; one of them just mashed dough.

I don't know Japanese.

HOHN-goh wah, wah-KAH-ree-mah-shen

Hoh, go wash—wash Carry, my son.

Envision an American trying to mime the above phrase, because he doesn't know Japanese.

Second Interlude

One of the attributes of learning memory techniques is that you don't have to rush. The more time you spend learning these systems, the better you will be at applying memory systems to what you want to learn. So feel free to put the book aside for a while and rest, play, or practice what you've learned on nonacademic areas.

But before you put *The Student's Memory Book* aside, take a couple of seconds to review the following points. Let them filter through your conscious and subconscious minds.

1. Decide what information you want to learn, and which facts are important to know. Underline these points or make a separate list. Focus on the material you've selected and ignore everything else.

2. Organize the material. Put the information into categories so that your associations are effortless and logical. Make stories out of the information you link together. Make analogies, *see* the similarities among the pieces of information, as well as the differences. Group the material so you have fewer things to remember.

7

Geography, World Affairs, and Where in the World Things Are

There's a cliché that goes something like this: If you don't know the rules, you can't play the game. While most clichés should be buried in a linguistic graveyard, this one makes considerable sense when it comes to geography and world affairs. If you don't know countries, capitals, rivers, and heads of states, you're going to have a great deal of trouble with these subjects.

Numerous locations and directions, such as "east" and "river" appear over and over again. Instead of creating a mnemonic each time you need to use east or river, it's worthwhile formulating a set of standard geographic mnemonics that you can call on whenever you want. The following list includes some (but not all) of the most commonly occurring places, objects, and directions. You may want to add to the list the information that you frequently encounter.

Adler's Common Geographic Mnemonic List

North	A great cloud with a face, blowing cold wind
South	A palm tree on a deserted island
East	The sun rising with great brilliance
West	The Wicked Witch of the West
United States	Uncle Sam
Africa	Elephant
Europe	The Concorde jet plane
China	The Great Wall of China
The USSR	A hammer and sickle
Asia	Lots of television sets, VCRs, and stereos
Arctic	Polar bear
Antarctic	Penguins
Italy	A boot with pasta in it
Australia	Lots of kangaroos
Egypt	The pyramids
Germany	Volkswagen
Israel	Star of David
An Arab country (in general)	Camels
Malta	A falcon
Panama	Panama hat
Switzerland	Watches and cuckoo clocks
India	Taj Mahal
Rome	The Coliseum with gladiators fighting inside

A kingdom	A crown or royal clothing
Britain	Warm beer, English muffin
Japan	Zeros (Japanese fighters from World War II), or Mount Fuji, or a Sony TV

Maps

Geography—indeed, anything having to do with countries, cities, politics, or the world—isn't just a matter of remembering names, places, or populations. Exactly where things appear on a map is usually important. If you don't know that Libya and Chad are neighbors, or that the shortest distance for ICBMs to travel between the USSR and United States is over the North Pole, or that the Falkland Islands are a considerable distance from Argentina, or that the Statue of Liberty is actually in New Jersey waters, not New York's, or that the White Cloud Mountains in Idaho are an extension of the Rocky Mountains, or that the Golan Heights in Israel, formerly part of Syria, overlook some of Israel's most productive kibbutzim, you won't be able to understand the intricacies of national or global politics. Where something is on a map can be just as important as who the country's leader is or what its principal export happens to be.

Learning where places are, relative to each other, is a difficult task. Even people who can name the capitals of all fifty states usually can't show you where in these states the capitals are located.

But there is a way of remembering detailed geographical information. To do this, superimpose a grid (Figure 1) on top of whatever map—be it a city, country, or world map—you want to learn. If you have already learned points on this grid, it's a simple matter to link points on the grid to the parts of map you want to learn.

Think of the grid as a chessboard. Each position on a chessboard can be represented in several ways, including the intersection of the horizontal and vertical axes.

Learning the grid—which can be applied to any kind of map, including an imaginary map of a parking lot so that you don't forget where you left your car—is easy to do. You already know all the mnemonics you need to apply this grid.

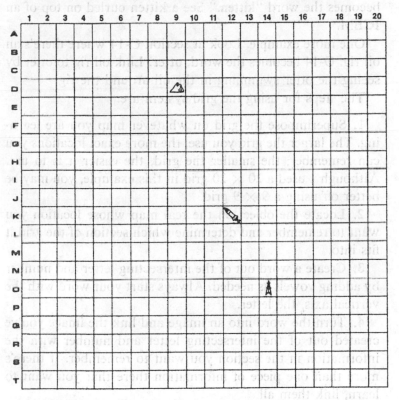

Notice that any section (box) on the map in Figure 1 can be expressed as the intersection of the horizontal and vertical axes. For example, the upper left hand corner is A-1; the lower right is T-20. To remember a particular section on the map you simply remember the corresponding letter and number. Perhaps you want to remember the section with the mountain in it, D-9. First, convert D-9 into a word by transposing 9 into its corresponding consonant, **p** (or b) and filling the space between the **p** and **D** with a vowel, i. So D-9 becomes **dip**. Second, link **dip** to the mountain; imagine a mountain being **dipped**.

Another example: the ICBM in section K-12. First, K-12 becomes the word "kitten." See a kitten curled on top of an ICBM.

One more example. Look at section O-14 where there's an oil rig. O-14 becomes the word, **otter**. Link oil rig to otter by seeing the otter swimming in the oil around the rig.

The steps for using the grid system are:

1. Superimpose the grid on whatever map you are learning. The larger the grid you use, the more exact locations you can remember; the smaller the grid, the easier it is to use. Although I used a 20 × 20 grid in this example, you may be better off using a 9 × 9 grid.

2. Locate the object on the real map whose location you want to remember and determine which section of the grid it fits into.

3. Create a word out of the intersecting letter and number by adding vowels as needed. Always start your word with the vertical axis, the letter.

4. Turn the word into an image and link the image you've created out of the intersecting letter and number with the information in the section you want to remember. If there's more than one piece of information there that you want to learn, link them all.

If you are going to be using maps a lot, take an hour and create a permanent mnemonic out of the intersecting letters and numbers for each of the sections on the grid. When you've established your grid images, all you will have to do then is link these images to what you want to remember.

Some Countries and Their Capitals

Below are some examples of mnemonics for countries.

Country   Afghanistan
Capital   Kabul
Languages   Pushtu and Dari Persian

An **afghan** dog in a **cab** with a **bull**. The cab is being pushed on a **persian** rug, because of a **dare**.

Country   Angola
Capital   Luanda
Languages   Portuguese (official), Bantu

Hanging a **goat** and waving a **wand** over it. The goat turns into a **Portuguese** man-of-war jellyfish which is, itself, **bantering**.

Country   Argentina
Capital   Buenos Aires
Language   Spanish

Oranges that are **tiny** get **blown** in the **air**.

Country   Australia
Capital   Canberra
Language   English

The **last straw** was when the **English**man stole the **can of berries** from (for good measure) the **Australian**.

Country   Austria
Capital   Vienna
Language   German

A **straw** was found in the **Vienna** sausage by **Herman**.

Country   Canada
Capital   Ottawa
Languages   English, French

Can add an otter to those cold, **Canadian** rivers.

Country   Haiti
Capital   Port-au-Prince
Languages   French, Creole
Visualize people (your image of Haitians) **hating** the **prince**
who's at the **port**. Or they hate the prince for drinking all the
port (wine) and leaving them none.

Country   Honduras
Capital   Tegucigalpa
Language   Spanish
Someone **gulping** down a **Honda** motorcycle.

Country   Hungary
Capital   Budapest
Language   Hungarian
A **hungry** Hungarian; that is, a Hungarian who is sitting next
to a bowl of goulash, but who isn't allowed to eat it. The
Hungarian's kid brother is playing with his **buddha** statue
and being a **pest**.

Country   Swaziland
Capital   Mbabane
Languages   English and Siswati
My Bonnie lies—well, over the ocean, but in a **land** that is
swaying.

Country   Sweden
Capital   Stockholm
Language   Swedish
Sweeten the **stock** of food for **home**.

Country   Tunisia
Capital   Tunis
Languages   Arabic, French
Tuning your **knees** with a tuning fork; then covering them
with a **tunic** for protection.

Country   Turkey
Capital   Ankara
Language   Turkish

A **turkey** being used instead of an **anchor**; the boat that is practicing this unusual procedure is moored off the coast of Turkey, a country populated by turkeys wearing clothing.

Country   United Kingdom
Capital   London
Language   English

Visualize plenty of **kingdoms**—the fanciful, Disneyland kind —tied together; rising up in the center of these kingdoms is the Tower of **London**. Alternatively, you might use the symbol for England, warm beer (beer with steam rising from it), and have the beer being poured into the River Thames in London.

Country   United States
Capital   Washington, D.C.
Language   English

Uncle Sam is the symbol for the United States; this symbol can be employed in a myriad of circumstances. Make sure that your image of Uncle Sam is detailed and stylized. I *always* envision him with his hand and finger outstretched as in the Army poster and all of the ads that mimic it. To remember that Washington is the capital of the United States, visualize Uncle Sam helping George Washington off the boat after Washington crosses the Delaware.

Country   Vietnam
Capital   Hanoi
Language   Vietnamese

A **veterinarian named** Spot would be very **annoy**ing.

8

Mathematics

So far, every subject that had seemed difficult to memorize has been easy. The same is true for one of the most frightening subjects, mathematics.

To begin, let's quickly jump into an equation and learn how to memorize it. Here's something that looks particularly nasty, something that could actually produce drops of sweat: representing vector algebra. Vector algebra equations are tedious and confusing to learn, unless you use mnemonics. The symbol for a vector quantity is $\vec{A}$, which we will think of as an A-frame house. This image needs to be linked to "vector," so let's do that. A vector is a kind of direction, and often the bar on top of the letter is an arrow, ———>. Whenever a bar or arrow is on top of a letter, it represents vector quantity. See an arrow piercing the A-frame house.

Because vector is a kind of direction, it can be expressed as a sum of the components of Cartesian coordinates:

$$\vec{A} = \vec{a}_x A_x + \vec{a}_y A_y + \vec{a}_z A_z$$

This expression is easier to remember than it looks. On one of the platters of a scale place the A-frame with the arrow through it. Let's break the different parts of the right side of the equation into manageable parts. A_x becomes **ax**; A_y becomes **eye**; and A_z becomes **ooze**. The $\vec{a}$ components of this equation are small versions of the above objects—a small ax next to a large ax, a small eye next to a large eye, and a small amount of ooze next to an unfortunately large amount of ooze. The small quantities have arrows through them. If you want, you can transform this image into a story.

That's it. This may seem like a strange way to memorize math, but it probably works faster than anything else you've ever learned. Most likely it took a full minute for you to develop this picture—not long for an equation, and not long for a technique you're unfamiliar with. But now for the pudding part. Take a twenty-minute break. Then resurrect the equation from your brain's memory cells. You'll discover that you remember it perfectly.

There are standard mnemonic images that can be used to represent the most common mathematical expressions. These equivalents may, of course, be tempered with your imagination.

Adler's Practical Guide to Remembering Math Symbols

In those cases where I have provided more than one image for a particular mathematical symbol, select only *one* image for that symbol (or create your own) and use that image all the time. By relying on a specific image, you won't confuse that image with anything else.

=   seesaw; balance scale (as in the scales of justice); railroad tracks. Note that you don't always need to have an equals sign in your mnemonic; simply connecting the two parts of the equation may be sufficient.

—   sword; belt buckle; something being left behind; holes in pockets; eyelash; 100-meter dash

+   superglue; stapled together; holding hands; a cross; crosshairs in a rifle sight; a star twinkling; fastened together in any fashion

×   the New York *Times*; rabbits multiplying; a machine that miraculously turns a few of an object into many; a supernova anything that happens many times; X marks the spot on a pirate's map; X ray, helicopter (the blades are like an X)

%   a windmill; two balloons attached to the same stick; eyeglasses; a **purse** with a **cent** in it

a   an apple

A (as opposed to little a)   an A-frame house

b   bee

c   a sea; a collar or necklace; cow

d   dog

f   frog

g   giraffe

h   hippopotamus

i (imaginary numbers)   igloo; ghostly-looking numbers; an eye

j   a fishhook (looks like a fishhook)

n   nun

y   a forked tongue; fireplace prongs; a divining rod; yo-yo

z   zebra; laser beam (zap)

! (factorial)   An ice-cream cone (that's what it looks like); a raindrop (also a visual relationship); an eyebrow

/ or ÷ (division)   a roadblock (symbolic in more ways than one); file cabinet (for dividing things); knife; jail cells (or anything that represents division); alternatively, you could simply place the numerator on top of the denominator in your image.

√ (square root) a hollowed-out root

square (power of 2) a caret (a square is represented on a personal computer by the caret symbol, ^); nerd (a square person); a picture frame; an actual □

roots to other powers a hollowed-out root with the picture representing that power embedded in it. For example, for the cube root, a ham stuck to the root would suffice.

exponents to other powers squares (carets, etc.) with the picture representing that number attached to the square. For example, the fifth power would be represented by a hook holding up a picture frame; a great power such as an explosion or supernova. **Exponent** in general can be represented by **raising** with a crane or pulley

log a log

ε (natural logarithm) a log on display in a museum; a Pac-Man game piece (looks kind of like an e)

sine sinning; a road sign (sine) with trigonometric equations on it

tangent tanning; a neighbor (as in tangent to); a tan gent

cosine a costar (also sinning, perhaps); a $—cosine can sound like cost

cotangent a coat

arc tangent, arc sine, arc cosine the previous images bent into an arc; the previous images with wings, as in archangel

θ (theta) egg with a belt

Σ (summation of) sleeping (the zzzzzs); a maze

∫ (integral) a lightning bolt; Superman (the S on his chest); a racetrack

$\frac{dy}{dx}$ (the derivative of y with respect to x, frequently expressed as y′) a distance (many FM receivers have a button marked DX, which stands for distance); dance; water moving through a pipe (derivates have to do with rates of change); a dirigible

π (pi)   a pie
Δ (delta)   a pyramid
———>   arrow
0   a hose (from the number system, if it's appropriate); a ring
1   a hat from the mnemonic system; a **pen**
negative numbers   numbers encased in ice; numbers under the ocean—below sea level
hypotenuse   hippopotamus
side opposite   a playground slide (notice the angle and notice underside of the slide)
side adjacent   a ladder leaning at an angle
lim (limit)   a lime; a dead end
$_x$ (subscript)   subscript attached to the lower part of the object; the two linked with a submarine (boat or sandwich)
^{x} (superscript)   superscript attached to the upper part of the object; a super-looking script (handwriting)
. (decimal point)   When the decimal point occurs to the right or left of the digits, you can usually ignore it. When it is in the middle of the number, create two different words on either side of the decimal point and separate those numbers with a pit or some other object that closely resembles a decimal point.

In mathematical equations, if there is no mnemonic given then assume that the adjacent images (numerals) are to be multiplied together. A bunch of mathematical mnemonics linked together without a mnemonic for an operation are all multiplied. For example, if you have a hair sticking out of a **pie** next to an X, then assume that that stands for $4\pi X$.

Trigonometry

In trigonometry, as with most areas of mathematics, it's best to select a particular image to represent a mathematical symbol, and to use that image for that symbol all the time. Just as π is always represented by a pie, and Σ by sleeping or a maze (but only one at a time), the elements of trigonometric equations will also be composed of a single image.

$$\sin = \frac{a}{c} = \frac{\text{opposite side}}{\text{hypotenuse}}$$

An **A.C.**; (for $\frac{a}{c}$) an air conditioner; **sin**ning. There's a hippopotamus standing beneath a playground slide. You can equate $\frac{a}{c}$ with hypotenuse opposite side by placing them on a seesaw.

$$\cos = \frac{b}{c} = \frac{\text{adjacent side}}{\text{hypotenuse}}$$

Visualize dollar bills being traded by cave dwellers in **B.C.** (for $\frac{b}{c}$). The cave dwellers are trying to get their dollars to a safe place, so they place a ladder over a hippopotamus.

$$\tan = \frac{a}{b} = \frac{\text{opposite side}}{\text{adjacent side}}$$

The alphabet is waiting in line at a **tan**ning parlor. Only two letters can get in at a time, and of course that's A and B, who are presently enjoying their **tan**. The rest of the letters are occupying their time by gliding down the slide; to get on the slide, they need to climb a ladder.

$$\text{cotangent} = \frac{b}{a} = \frac{\text{adjacent side}}{\text{opposite side}}$$

There's a coat being worn **back**ward. It looks funny, as does climbing up the slide only to walk down the ladder, also a backward action. Everything about cotangent is backward: See the action happening.

To remember that "a" is the side opposite, see a playground slide supported by **A**-frames. To remember that "b" is the side adjacent, visualize **b**ees swarming around a ladder. Finally to remember that "c" is the hypotenuse, see a hippo wandering in a murky sea, as hippos are wont to do. (Or you might envision a hippo with a c-shaped collar around its neck.)

Calculus

Is it possible that all of calculus can be reduced to simple mnemonic techniques? Well, the reasoning behind equations can't be, but the most fundamental principles and expressions can be, making the rest of this much-taught branch of mathematics easier to cope with. (Whew.)

Let's start with the most basic expression in calculus:

$$\frac{dy}{dx} = \lim \Delta x \longrightarrow 0 \ \frac{\Delta y}{\Delta x}$$

All of which is pronounced: the derivative of y with respect to x is equal to the rate of change of y with respect to x. But you don't need to know that to memorize this equation; you don't even need to know what it means to remember it. (In fact, the meaning of this equation and others is relatively irrelevant to this book.)

So to learn this equation, imagine a **dirigible** balanced on a seesaw; on the other side a **lime** balanced on top of a **pyramid** and buttressed by a more sensible support, an X. An **arrow** is fired from their direction right through a ring.

A simple, though slightly strange, story. But as strange as it is, it is certainly easier than remembering symbols like Δx.

Another basic expression in differential calculus solves the derivative of exponents and is resolved this way:

$$\frac{dx^n}{dx} = nx^{n-1}$$

We've encountered $\frac{dy}{dx}$, the derivative of y with respect to x, before, but not $\frac{dx}{dx}$; dx in the upper portion of the fraction simply stands for any number, and dx^n means the derivative of any number to any exponent—positive, negative, integral, fractional, or irrational with respect to x. It's essentially the same thing as dy, except that the exponent is the important consideration in this case. So start with $\frac{dx^n}{dx}$, which can be represented by a dirigible with an explosion taking place in part of it. See the dirigible on one side of the seesaw. On the other side, envision another explosion knocking a helicopter over; the **helicopter** is being hoisted by a **nun** who is so busy her **pen** is being held in her **eyelash**.

Linear Algebra

Other advanced mathematics can just as easily be memorized with these mnemonic systems. Let's take a look at an example, the equation for an inverted 2 × 2 matrix:

$$A^{1} = ad - \frac{1}{bc} \begin{vmatrix} d & -b \\ -c & a \end{vmatrix}$$

where A^{-1} is called an invertible matrix.

The first step in conquering this formula is to create a mnemonic for A^{1} as an invertible matrix. See an A-frame house turned upside down—that is, inverted. Put the inverted A-frame on the seesaw. On the other side put an apple in a dog's mouth (remember, where there is no mnemonic for an operator, assume that the relationship between the two objects is multiplication). See a huge eyelash (for —) on the dog. Alighting on the dog's eyelash is a bee, which the dog is not too crazy about. There's a collar around the bee's neck.

Meanwhile, the dog is trying to get into the matrix, for which we also need a mnemonic. A jungle gym will work well for matrix.

The dog is climbing the jungle gym to escape the bee. Inside the gym, the matrix, we have to place various symbols in their correct positions. (Keep in mind that what we are doing here is creating a memory device for a general formula which can be applied to numerous examples.)

The letters inside the matrix have specific positions. So far we've been learning to remember information in a relativistic fashion—that is, where an object is in relation to other objects. But this can grow confusing and complicated, especially as the systems, such as matrices, become larger. What we need to do is establish an overall system to use when items have to be placed in a particular location. For a 2 × 2 matrix, what we want to do is define each of the four spaces in the matrix permanently and then link the variables to those spaces. That way you can respond quickly and correctly to the question, "What number is in the lower right-hand corner of such-and-such matrix?"

Think of the matrix as a map with four possible locations that can be pinpointed by the intersection of the x and y axes. If we place letters across the x axis and numbers across the y axis and then link the two, we can make a unique word *and picture* for each location by linking the number and letter that form the intersection for a particular component of the matrix.

$$\begin{array}{c} & A & B \\ 1 & d & -b \\ 2 & -c & a \end{array}$$

If the words we create always start with the consonant represented by the number, then each space in the matrix becomes quickly identifiable. The only rule involved is that each word be no more than four letters long. Thus the spot occupied by the **d** becomes **tap**. Link tap to dog—a dog doing a tap dance—and you'll remember where the **d** goes. The location of the **−b** is identified by **tab**. Find a bee with heavy eyebrows (the sign for minus sign) drinking a **tab**. The **−c** position is **nap**; see a **c**ow with bushy eyebrows taking a nap. The last variable, a, is identified by the location **knob**. See a knob in the shape of an **a**pple (for a).

See all of this inside the jungle gym.

This mapping system can be applied to any size matrix; just place more letters along the horizontal axis, and continue the numbers along the vertical axis. (The chapter on geography covers mapping in more detail, and provides some examples that will enhance your ability to structure matrices in your mind.)

That's it. With this system, you can remember a matrix of any complexity.

9

Economics

Economics is a much easier subject when you understand
what's going on. To help accomplish that, I've devoted most
of this chapter to creating mnemonics for terms used frequently in economics courses. Once you've learned these—a
swift process—you will have no trouble understanding and
memorizing economics. Toward the end of the chapter are
some examples of how to apply these mnemonics.

The material in this chapter closely follows the information in Paul Samuelson's textbook *Economics*. In addition to
enhancing your memory, this chapter will give you an advantage in economics courses.

GLOSSARY: KEY ECONOMIC TERMS

Assets Asses (the donkey kind) carrying bags filled with gold. Notice that this image has both a semantic and phonetic link to the word assets.

Collusion A **collision** of two companies: the entire companies collide, with disastrous consequences, of course.

Competition Two runners competing in a race. But these are not your ordinary runners: they are two candy bars with arms, legs, and heads, and are dressed like runners, competing. I've selected a Hershey and a Nestlé's Crunch bar as the runners for my image, but you can certainly pick any you want.

Capital The U.S. Capital (or the U.S. Mint).

Capitalism A baseball **cap** with a dollar sign on the front. (Baseball is American and so is capitalism.)

Consumer Price Index Consumers (shoppers, in curls, with tote bags) being placed in a filing cabinet—indexed.

Cost Cast. (A phonetic mnemonic.)

Debt An individual receiving all his bills—phone, rent, utilities, credit cards—at the same moment.

Dollar A dollar bill that is flying through the air like a bird.

Deflation A bag of money, deflating.

Demand A demon. (Demon has both an auditory and semicontextual resemblance to demand, if you think of demand as being demonic.)

Depression A canyon—a large **depression**.

Diminishing Returns, Law of A very small "Returns" counter in a department store.

Disposable Income A garbage can, the sole purpose of which is to collect unwanted dollar bills.

Division of Labor Half-workers; that is, the left or right sides of workers.

Distribution Envision trucks leaving a central location and heading across America's highways in divers directions. Make this image stylized.

Economy A soda-vending machine. This is a fairly arbitrary selection to represent economy, but it is not without merit. A vending machine does represent many of the principles of an economy in a small space and it is easy to remember. If you want to create your own image for economy, be sure not to make the connection between economy and that image too abstract.

Economic Man A little man coming out of a soda-vending machine.

Efficiency Someone quickly and perfectly cleaning a room (dorm room, apartment, office, whatever).

Elasticity A very strong rubber band that does not break no matter how much stress is put on it.

Equilibrium An aquarium. Besides having a similar sound, unless an aquarium is in equilibrium, the fish will die.

Economies of Scale Two vending machines balanced on either side of a scale.

Equity A railroad track (looks like an equals sign).

Equity Capital A railroad track running through the U.S. Capital.

Escalator Clause Santa Claus riding up an escalator.

Excise Tax Exercising with tacks (should create a fairly memorable image).

Exports Pushing objects out of the ports of ships.

Float An ice-cream float.

Floating Exchange Rate Visualize **floating change**.

Foreign Exchange Lots of strange, **foreign change**.

Free Trade See **Trade**. Two little boys **trading** baseball cards, but these boys are not normal: they are **freaks**. (Free trade also happens to be a freak phenomenon.)

Final Good See **Goods**. An assembly line that produces products with smiley faces. However, there's only one, **final** good left on the assembly line. (Thank goodness.)

Fixed (as in fixed cost) Something (whatever is fixed) with Band-Aids covering it. So "fixed cost" would be a cracked cast (cost) repaired with Band-Aids.

Full Employment Envision an unemployment center with plenty of clerks, but no unemployed people in line.

Goods Products with yellow, smiley faces.

GNP (Gross National Product) Grocery store.

Inflation A money bag being **inflated**.

Income People **coming** into your home with money for *you*.

Internal Revenue Service A horrible, human-eating dragon monster that's oozing out green slime through its skin and baring grizzly teeth. This monster also has an appetite for cash.

Indifference Curve A special type of baseball pitch that nobody cares about; the spectators yawn when it's thrown. (An indifference curve yields the points at which consumers are satisfied.)

Inelastic Somebody wearing underwear with worn-out elastic.

Inferior Good Goods sold in the bargain basement of a store. Really stylize this image.

Innovation A factory inside of a weather **vane**.

Investment A **vest** with **mints** as buttons.

Invisible Hand An invisible hand inside of a glove.

Labor Force An army of workers carrying their tools.

Labor Supply Thousands of workers with their tools in a truck.

Laissez-faire A lazy fairy.

Land Kansas wheatfields on top of New England apple orchards, on top of Florida's beaches on top of California vineyards.

Liabilities Lying butterflies.

Long Run A marathon race.

Marginal Cost **Margarine** on a **cast**.

Marginal Product **Margarine** spilled on top of **produce**.

Marginal Utility **Margarine** melting on top of a **utility** pole.

Market A market, preferably the free-wheeling Middle Eastern type.

Marxism The Marx brothers (or just one).

Mercantilism   A **mercury**-covered **cantaloupe**.

Mixed Economy   Shaking a soda-vending machine, or mixing it up.

Money   An animated dollar sign ($), with arms, legs, and a head.

Money Supply   A truckload of these $-creatures.

Monopoly   The board game Monopoly.

Multiplier   A gadget that is not one, but multiple pliers in a single tool.

Output   Outboard motor.

Poverty   Picture the South Bronx, Appalachia, Calcutta—the image of poverty should be easy enough to find in your mind.

Present Value   A valuable-looking present, perhaps with gold gift wrapping that glitters.

Price   Prize ice has a purple ribbon around it. Prize ice, as you know, also commands a high price.

Productivity   **Producing ducks**.

Profit   A man in sackcloth preaching on a street corner.

Protectionism   Cops standing on the border of the United States (actually see them standing on a giant map's border), keeping foreign goods out.

Real Wages   **Reeling in waves**.

Regulation   A valve on a furnace.

Resource   A **racehorse**.

Revenue   A **river view**.

Savings   A piggy bank.

Short Run   A sprint.

Stagflation   A male deer with wings.

Stock   Stock certificates.

Stock Market   Envision the floor of the stock market, or create an image of the old-fashioned stock ticker.

Subsidy   Suds.

Substitutes   Submarines.

Supply   A slide.

Tariff A **towel**, preferably one that's not made in the U.S.A.

Tax **Tacks**.

Trade Two little boys trading baseball cards.

Total Bowl of Total cereal.

Underground Economy Soda-vending machines located underground.

Unemployment A packed unemployment center.

Variable (as in variable cost) A fairy (which, in addition to sounding somewhat like "variable," changes frequently, as does a fairy). So variable cost would be a cast with fairies dancing on it.

Velocity of Money Those little $-creatures in race cars moving along very quickly.

Wealth Rich whales dressed in fine silks with jewelry, and wearing sunglasses.

APPLICATIONS OF ECONOMIC MNEMONICS

Now to apply these terms to more complicated economic notions.

Acceleration Principle

An investment spending theory which maintains that the level of investment will be governed by the rate of increase in the Gross National Product. So even when the GNP is high, if it is steady there will be little or no net investment.

Visualize a car with silver dollars as wheels, accelerating. Inspect the speedometer in your mind, if you want; see it moving from zero to sixty in no time. Now construct an image for Gross National Product, GNP. The best visual representation for GNP that I can think of is a grocery store (there's a phonetic and semantic similarity between "Gross" and "grocery") stocked with not just fruits and other foods, but with every conceivable product—TVs, medicines, books, clothing, kitchen sinks.

See the car drive into the grocery store, fill up on the store's wares, and then **accelerate** out. Be sure you see the speedometer as it accelerates. If you can't create a strong image for acceleration, substitute a more concrete picture for it based on that word's sounds. An **ax** cutting **celery** will remind you of accelerate.

Beggar-Thy-Neighbor Policy

A government policy of "exporting" a country's unemployment by imposing quotas or tariffs on foreign imports to increase demand for domestic goods, and thus the amount of work for domestic workers.

This mnemonic will be entirely scene-oriented. Picture two adjacent countries—the United States and Mexico will do. Conjure a fence between the two nations through which trading occurs. You might see TVs, tortillas, or baseball cards changing hands. On the U.S. side of the fence there's prosperity—big houses, swimming pools, fancy cars; on the Mexican side is poverty—straw huts, malnourished children, dusty streets. The Mexicans construct a more formidable wall where the fence once stood, making it more difficult for U.S. products to enter. Perhaps there's a customs station the Mexicans are manning, restricting U.S. products but allowing their own to pass through freely.

That image will let you remember the concept, but now comes the key part, linking the concept to the definition, because it's most likely that you will have to retrieve the information when cued by its definition: see a **beggar** carrying the Mexican goods to the United States, and not being allowed to cross the other way with products for sale.

Capital Deepening

When growth in the real capital stock occurs at a faster rate than the rate of increase of the total labor force, which leads to an increase in the ratio of capital to labor.

This is a bit of a mouthful, guaranteed to appear in one

form or another in an exam. It's a fairly straightforward proposition to create an image for the definition of capital deepening: picture laborers (economists, if you like) digging a deep hole using a shovel fashioned out of paper money or quarters.

There's money at the bottom of the well. They add more laborers to the effort, and the deeper the hole gets, the more money they find. In fact, they can't get enough workers to dig deeply or quickly enough—they produce money at a faster rate than they need additional workers.

Cobweb Theorem

A changing model of supply and demand in which nonrational desires lead to perpetual oscillations in prices. Some economists believe that this applies to agricultural markets.

Cobwebs are easy enough to visualize—but what do they have to do with economics? (It's always fortunate when part of what you want to remember has an image built into its name, like cobweb.)

First, break down this definition into its meaningful parts —that is, the parts you are going to have to remember and have trouble remembering. "Nonrational desires," "perpetual oscillations," and "prices" are the key words. For nonrational desires, imagine a **nun ration**ing her **desserts**. Perhaps she is meticulously wrapping them in Ziplock plastic bags, marking each with a date. (A nun rationing her desires would not be a good image because you would still have the problem of converting "desires" into a tangible image or sound. Dessert sounds like desire, and frequently is a desire.)

For perpetual oscillations there are several possibilities, but I will offer only one. You could color the cobweb **purple** and make it oscillate back and forth, thus establishing the link between the definition and defined word. To remember prices, establish a link between the purple, oscillating cobweb and **prize ice**—see the prize ice (with a purple ribbon around it and everything) bouncing up and down on the purple, oscillating cobweb.

The only remaining task is to connect our nun to the cobweb, which is straightforward enough: either the nun or her desserts become stuck in the cobweb.

Derived Demand

The demand for a product that is derived from the demand for the ultimate good which it contributes to. For example, the demand for gasoline stems from the demand for automobiles.

An **ivy**-covered demon that has grown out of the stem of another ivy-covered demon.

Duopoly

A market in which there are only two sellers.

Envision just that: a market in which there are only two sellers. Others try to enter the market, but can't.

Income Effect (Decrease)

A lessening in the demand for a product because the increase in the commodity's price lowers the consumer's real income.

Envision demons coming into your home carrying money —$-signs with arms and legs flailing about. As the moments pass, there are fewer and fewer demons entering. The reason fewer and fewer demons can enter is because there is **prize ice** blocking the door and the ice is getting bigger and bigger. Naturally, if there are fewer demons coming in with money, the consumer has less income.

Graphs, Curves, and Formulas

Among the most common figures in economics are graphs, specifically curves and lines. In fact, some people say that if you can master the graphs in economics, you have the subject beaten.

But how do you remember all those straight or not-so-straight lines? Not to mention the intersections of those lines, which seem to be all-important when it comes to econ exams. Actually, remembering information contained in graphs is easier than learning just about any other kind of material.

Let's start with a basic supply-and-demand graph, which is supposed to tell us something about price. See Figure 1. In this generalized graph, notice the line that is tilting downward to the right, and the second line, the upward-tilting line, which is the supply curve. Where they intersect—$95 and 71 units—gives us the optimal price point and unit supply respectively.

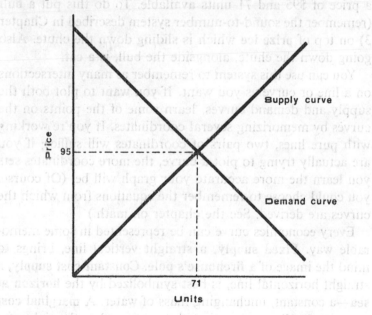

So how do we learn all that? Easily, of course.

First, establish an image that represents the market demand curve here. Maybe a demand curve reminds you of a mountain slope—both angle steeply down (especially if you have vertigo). To remember that the demand curve slopes downward to the right, think that going **down** the **mountain** is the **right** thing to do. So from now on a **demand curve** is a **mountain slope**.

For the supply curve: A chute should work adequately, especially the kind of chute that finished products in an assembly line slide down. From now on a **supply curve** is represented by a **chute**.

To remember that you're focusing on the intersection of a supply-and-demand curve, see a chute crossing a mountain slope.

That's not all you need to know, of course. You need to remember that the intersection of these two curves occurs at a price of $95 and 71 units available. To do this put a **bull** (remember the sound-to-number system described in Chapter 3) on top of **prize ice** which is sliding down the chute. Also going down the chute, alongside the bull, is a **cat**.

You can use this system to remember as many intersections on a line or curve as you want. If you want to plot both the supply and demand curves, learn some of the points on the curves by memorizing several coordinates. If you're working with pure lines, two pairs of coordinates will suffice; if you are actually trying to plot a curve, the more coordinates sets you learn the more accurate your graph will be. (Of course, you could choose to remember the equations from which the curves are derived. See the chapter on math.)

Every economics curve can be represented in some memorable way. **Fixed supply**, a straight vertical line, brings to mind the image of a **firehouse's pole**. **Constant-cost supply**, a straight horizontal line, is best symbolized by the **horizon at sea**—a constant, unchanging mass of water. A **marginal cost** curve, normally a curve that slopes upward to the right at a 40-degree angle or so, can be remembered by a knife leaning against a stick of **margarine**.

Formulas can be remembered in a similar—dare I say "pleasant?"—manner. Let's look at a couple of examples that will pave the way to being able to remember any economics formula you want. All of these examples are used in Paul Samuelson's *Economics,* so if you are using that text you will quickly become a whiz in class. You don't have to know the meaning of these formulas in order to remember them, but the more you know the easier it is. The first formula is AC = $\frac{TC}{q}$ = AFC + AVC, where AC is average cost, TC is total cost, q is output, AFC is average fixed cost, and AVC stands for average variable costs. For average cost, substitute an **air conditioner,** an **AC.** For total cost see a plaster **cast** in a bowl of **Total** cereal. To remember that total cost is divided by output, see an outboard motor churning the cereal around, only it's churning so quickly that the cereal is being **divided,** like the parting of the Red Sea. To equate these two items, place them on opposite sides of a seesaw, which stands for equals. Anthropomorphize if you want. (A seesaw balances things, just as an equals sign does. See the chapter on mathematics for quick mnemonic devices to use to memorize mathematical expressions.) There's a third part to this equation, AVC + AFC. Average variable cost can be remembered through seeing **average**-looking fairies dancing on a cast; average fixed cost's mnemonic is **a fudge** smeared all over a bandage-covered cast. Place these two different casts in the middle of the seesaw; they're for balancing the seesaw.

Another equation: V = $\frac{\$N}{i}$, which translates into the present value (V) equals permanent annual receipts ($N) divided by the interest rate (i, in decimal terms).

Again, we'll use a seesaw to balance the two sides of this equation. On one end of the seesaw place a valuable present (use your imagination to conjure the specific image—just make sure it's a present by including gift wrapping and a ribbon in your scene). On the other side of the seesaw see a nun (the image for the symbol n; again, see the chapter on mathematics for a complete listing of these symbols) clutching a $ (either the symbol or a dollar bill) in her hands, kind of like the eagle in the Great Seal clutching arrows. An **eye**

(i) is focusing on the nun, revealing a type of laser beam (the eye has a interest in her, too), and, as a consequence, the nun divides.

Ready for another equation? The "fundamental relation of growth accounting" equation is: % **Q growth** $= \frac{3}{4}$ (% **L growth**) $+ \frac{1}{4}$ (% **K growth**) $+$ **T.C.** Some definitions of the above before memorization commences:

% Q growth is growth in output
% L is percent labor
% K is percent capital
T.C. is technical change, or total factor productivity

As you've already noticed, there are generally three types of mimicry that can be performed on abstract symbols like **Q** or **%**. Not all these techniques work for everything you want to memorize. First, you can take the item you want to remember, translate and manipulate its shape into a memorable image. For example, % can become eyeglasses or a windmill.

The second possibility is to convert the *sound* of what you are trying to memorize from a nonsensical combination of sounds to a tangible object, objects, or action. In this way, % becomes a **purse** with a **cent** in it.

The third alternative is to take the *meaning* of that symbol, and use the meaning to create a tangible image. Unfortunately, not every symbol's meaning is readily converted into a memorable image: this is especially true for % and Q. However, the meaning of the symbol divide (/), can be easily converted into a picture: Imagine something being divided, or the Red Sea dividing.

Enough of this interlude. Back to the equation. The first step is to create a memorable image for Q growth, or growth in output. Several possibilities come to mind, and as always it's best to select the one that works most effectively for you. Everyone's imagination is different, and everyone is going to develop different images. So use the images in this book only if they work well for you; otherwise make your own.

For Q growth, growth in output, you can certainly imagine a **Q** growing out of the ground, or an **O** growing a leg, so it becomes a **Q**. Since you're making an equation with this Q, put the Q growing out of the ground on one end of the see-saw.

The alternative approach involves focusing not on the symbol, Q growth, but rather on the abstraction, "growth in output." Again, there are several ways of remembering this. You could see a **Q** growing out of an outboard motor (outboard motor, you recall from the list of economics definitions, is the image for output). If you aren't crazy about that Q-growing stuff, see the outboard motor on the seesaw: it's growing, getting bigger and heavier—and you know what happens when there are heavy items on one side of a seesaw.

Next step, $\frac{3}{4}$ (%L growth). Three fourths, hmm. You could visualize that someone ate $\frac{3}{4}$ of your dessert; perhaps you once had four cubes of Jell-O and now you only have one. Or you could see yourself (miraculously) dancing in $\frac{3}{4}$ time. Alternatively, there's the old standby of making images of the numbers themselves: the 3 becomes a ham and the 4 becomes a hair—a ham is **divided** by a hair. Use the hair like dental floss to divide the ham. Next step, relating what's outside to what is inside the parentheses. As you recall from math, any time a number or symbol is placed outside parentheses and there is no other connector such as a + or / between that number and what's inside the parentheses, the two are multiplied. Put that notion in the back of your head for the moment while we focus on what's inside the parentheses, (%L growth), percent in labor growth. You could see thousands of laborers (workers) wearing gigantic glasses, to fit into the glasses the workers are growing.

See the workers using the hair (again, like a dental floss) to cut the ham. As they cut the ham, rabbits (the symbol for multiplication) pop out. Or you might see a helicopter (another symbol for X) lifting the divided hams.

Phew. Not much more to go.

All right—that action gets added to $\frac{1}{4}$ (%K growth). For one fourth, you could conjure the image of a **quarter**, one quarter: a solitary quarter, with no change around. Or, instead of a quarter, you might want to translate the 1 and 4 into real images: The 1 is a hat, the 4 a hair—see a single hair sticking out of a hat like a feather. (Notice that we didn't do anything about division here; your intuition will know that the 1 and 4 should be related by division, $\frac{1}{4}$ rather than 14. You don't have to memorize every bit of information to learn something; your brain will fill in the gaps when they occur.) See rabbits coming out of the hat and into the U.S. Capitol Building. (Again, refer to the math chapter; rabbits also stand for multiplication.) Percent capital growth (%K growth) can be pictured by a **purse** pouring **cents** onto the U.S. **Capitol**; the cents are causing the Capitol to grow. Put the hat with its hair on top of the Capitol dome.

T.C., technical change, needs an image. You could see a golf **tee** on a **sea**.

Connect $\frac{1}{4}$ (%K growth) to T.C. by stapling the golf tee to the U.S. Capitol. (*Plus,* addition, can be turned into a mnemonic in various ways including staples, superglue, or a twinkling star.) With a big dollop of superglue attach workers by their feet to the Capitol. And put all that on the one end of the seesaw. Because all that weighs so much, the only way to equalize the two sides of the seesaw is to make the outboard (or Q) grow.

Quite a mouthful, I admit, but there's a virtue to all of these machinations: You know the equation!

Third Interlude

Your memory at this stage should be far better than you could ever have imagined. Put the book aside and take a break. You've earned it—and you can afford it. Let the information and skills you've acquired percolate through your subconscious.

But before you close the book, I want to remind you of some occasionally elusive points:

1. Make your mnemonic images bold and detailed. Don't hold back on your imagination.

2. Pay attention to what you are trying to memorize.

3. Organize the material. Select what you want to learn and put it into sensible categories.

4. Review and repeat. Mnemonic aids are enhanced every time you review the image or association you've made.

Now rest.

10

Biology

As you've discovered by now, once you've mastered the basic memory techniques you can learn anything. And you've no doubt also discovered that once you've become handy with these basic skills—surprise seeing, the link, the cue, and learning numbers—memorizing information associated with one subject is pretty much the same as memorizing the facts associated with any other subject. Some subjects require different emphasis, however; physics involves using mathematical mnemonics, while learning the details of a Shakespeare play doesn't. Each subject requires that you apply different strategies to learning. A physics curriculum can be memorized in discrete segments and the material you learn doesn't all have to be integrated: optics, mechanics, and electromagnetism can be separate topics. On the other hand, you couldn't very well understand the plot of *Romeo and Juliet* if you didn't know something about Mr. Romeo and Ms. Juliet, not to mention Shakespeare. History is like that too; events are closely linked.

The strategies that apply to each subject can't be explained, just as you can't explain to someone how to ride a bicycle, make an omelet, do a differential equation, or make love if they've never done that before. Many memory tasks only become learned and appreciated by doing them. You learn subtleties and finesse, and fine-tune your techniques, by doing. You will acquire those skills by working through the examples in this chapter.

Cell Structure

Let's start with some of the most essential biological information, which, by the way, is interesting in its own right: the structure of the cell. There are eight structures present in all cells. To remember this list of eight items, use the Top Ten system.

But before you embark on memorizing the items on this list, you want to develop a cue for the list, so that when you are asked to name the eight components of every cell, your mind will immediately think *cell,* then see a cell, then skip to the information. The most obvious cue for this list is **cell.** Now you have two choices: you can either envision an actual cell in your mind's eye or you can use a prison cell. Select whichever comes to mind first—whichever presents itself first will be the one you recall fastest and most completely later.

But, given that it's best to choose whichever image first comes to your mind, there's another consideration to take into account: it's also better to select an image that bears a semantic or visual relationship to what you are trying to remember. An image of a giant cell, as in a science fiction movie, for example, will probably remind you more easily of a cell later on than a prison cell would. Still, a prison cell is easier to visualize because it's a more common image.

What to do? Always trust your own judgment when it comes to memory; when it feels right, it is. (There's another thing you can do as well: go and take a look at some pictures of cells. Seeing photos of the object you want to remember will dramatically enhance your ability to visualize it.)

The next step: how to link the cue, cell, with the information on the list? As always, there are plenty of possibilities, but the one that may be most effective is to connect "cell" to the first two pictures of the Top Ten system. In other words, associate a cell to a pen, the number 1, and to a swan, the number 2. Linking the cue to the first two on the Top Ten mnemonic parade will be more than sufficient to stimulate your recall; you certainly don't have to link "cell" with every Top Ten image. However, linking "cell" to just the first image, "pen," may not be enough to prompt you later. Linking "cell" to two items gives you double the memory potential with little extra effort.

1. The first structure in every cell is the *cell membrane,* a double membrane that surrounds the cell protoplasm. It serves to regulate the passage of liquids and gases into and out of the cell. Cellular reactions also take place on the membrane.

The first step is to connect **cell** to **pen**, so that we will have an effective cue for the information. Envision a pen piercing a cell—the cell emits a high-pitched scream. (If you used a prison cell to stand for cell, imagine the prison bars made of pens. Maybe there are cells locked inside the prison.) Next, identify what you want to remember about the cell membrane. Most important is that it surrounds the cell protoplasm and regulates the flow of liquids and gases. There's an image that will let you remember almost all the information at once: Visualize a fountain pen squirting ink at a cell. When the cell wants to, it allows the ink inside, but most of the time it doesn't. To learn the term "cell protoplasm" and to remember that this means all the other stuff that's inside the cell, see a **photo** on a **platter** inside the cell. And that's why the cell only wants a certain amount of ink, because it's just touching up the cell a bit. The ink is reacting with the cell membrane, turning it blue.

2. The second component of a cell is the **cytoplasm**, the protoplasm of cells, which is composed of medium-sized particles in suspension. These particles are the right size for cellular reactions to take place.

Reinforce the cue by linking swan (represents the number 2) to cell. A swan nibbling on a cell floating in a lake will work. Next—memorize. Connect cytoplasm to swan by seeing a **seat** in **place** in the middle of a cell. Take a second or two to see the seat in the cell. The seat is composed of **particle** boards, but when the swan sits on the particle boards it reacts because there are splinters—ouch!

3. The **nucleus** controls the activities of the cell. It contains the genetic material that regulates heredity, the chromosomes. The nucleus also contains the nucleolus, which plays a role in the synthesis of proteins.

Connect bird in flight, the image for the number 3, to something that will help you remember nucleus. If you can visualize a cell nucleus (terrific!), see it resting on top of a bird's wings. If not, see a **nuke** resting there. Notice the **control** panel on the nuke; notice also that somebody took the time to sew a cute little cover for the control panel made out of **jeans**. Open the nuclear bomb and you will see a **nook** with an **Opus** (the penguin) sitting in the nook. "Protein" is a fairly difficult image to conjure, so see Opus as a **preteen**.

4. The **nuclear membrane** is a double membrane that regulates the flow of materials in and out of the nucleus.

Link a sailboat (for number 4) to this idea by noticing that the sail, a membrane, is made of cellular material. Someone hurls a **nuke** at it, but the membrane is too strong and the nuke bounces away harmlessly.

5. The **endoplasmic reticulum** provides a transport mechanism between cell parts, as well as a surface on which reactions can take place.

Link hook, the image for number 5, to endoplasmic reticulum. To what? Just envision a **rectangle** at the **end** of a **plastic** cell, a toy cell. Have a child lift the cell with a toy hook. To remember that endoplasmic reticulum is an intercellular transport system, see the cell being lifted to one place, picking up some material—a crayon, cell-stuff, cement, whatever you think of—then being hoisted to another spot and transporting the material it picked up to the second location. Another image you could turn into a mnemonic involves seeing the cell lifted by the hook onto a train, plane, or truck—whatever stands for transportation in your mind.

6. Ribosomes are small bodies that are located either on the surface of the endoplasmic reticulum or freely in the cytoplasm. Protein synthesis occurs on the ribosomes.

To create a mnemonic for ribosomes, see **ribs** with **homes** on them. A bag of golf clubs (for 6) has fallen in front of a home and there are clubs all over the front steps. There's something happening in these homes: a **preteen** is being **made** up. Some ribs are wrapped at the **end** of the **plastic rectangles**; others are loose within a **cell**.

7. The **mitochondria** are called the "powerhouse" of cells. This is where food, especially glucose, is turned into energy.

Envision a **mat** with a **condo** on it precariously balanced on the edge of a cliff. There are people eating food, including sugar cubes, and as they eat more they become more **energetic**. (Alternatively, if you'll read the chapter on physics, you know that the mnemonic for energy is a cloud of light with lightning and sparkles; you can see this spewing forth from these diners' mouths.)

8. Vacuoles are storage bodies for minerals, water, and other material. (In unicellular organisms such as bacteria, vacuoles also aid in digestion and elimination.)

Connect "vacuole" to "snowman" (which represents the number 8) by seeing someone **vacuum**ing the **holes** in the snowman. Actually visualize the snow flying around. Inside the vacuum the snow turns to water; also bits of minerals (or **mini holes**) have collected in the vacuum.

Photosynthesis

No biology course is complete without a discussion of photosynthesis, the process by which plants manufacture foods. Plants convert carbon dioxide (CO_2) and water (H_2O) in conjunction with chlorophyll and sunlight into simple sugars, which serve to provide energy for them. The chemical reaction is:

$$6CO_2 + 6H_2O \xrightarrow[\text{chlorophyll}]{\text{sunlight}} C_6H_{12}O_6 + 6O_2$$

Carbon dioxide is obtained through the stomata (a part of the plant stem); water enters the plant through the soil. Sunlight provides energy. The sugar that is produced by the plant is used directly for food and is also converted into more complex molecules—starch for future consumption—and ultimately is drawn into plant tissues. Plants obtain other materials they need, such as minerals and nitrogen, from the soil.

You may have learned about photosynthesis several times before, starting with biology class in elementary school. Now you are going to learn about it for the last time:

Create a cue for photosynthesis: A plant taking a **photo** during the daytime. See the camera slung around the plant's "neck" and the plant holding the camera with its little leaf arms. But it's an old plant, and it has to be given oxygen, which enters through a mask attached to a tube in the plant's **stem at** an angle. The plant has other problems, too—acne.

See the zits and see its face covered with **Clearasil** (chloro-phyll). After it takes the photo, the plant gets lunch—a **sugar** cube that a passing horse dropped and left behind.

To remember the chemical formula, an inevitable part of the exam, we'll create a story, a kind of extended acronym. Hear and see this story:

A **sick** (6) **coat, too sick**. There's **water** on the coat, that's why. The coat gets **seasick**; it **ha**tes being **twelve** and keeps saying, "**Oh**, I'm **sick. Sick. Oh . . . to** sleep.

This phrase may sound a bit convoluted to your ear, but it is many times easier to remember than the actual formula, which is an amalgam of unrelated letters and numbers. There are other, more "systematic" ways to learn chemical formulas. Those techniques are explained in the chapter on chemistry. Still, creating stories based on the elements of a formula is an acceptable, and memorable, way to learn information. Your objective is to memorize the information; in mnemonics the means is not important, only the ends are.

Infectious Diseases and Antibiotics

Medicine has advanced with dizzying speed during the past decades. Since Fleming accidentally discovered penicil-lin, the first antibiotic, in 1928 when he noticed that some green mold was preventing the growth of a bacteria colony, antibiotic therapy has advanced phenomenally. However, there are some bacterial diseases that still can make us very sick or can kill. As you learn about these still deadly diseases, keep in mind that bacterial infections are completely different from viral diseases. Rabies, the flu, AIDS, and smallpox are caused by viruses—and while rabies, the flu, and smallpox can be prevented by a vaccine, once you have contracted these infections there is no cure. Antibiotics do not affect viruses.

When **tetanus** was common it was called lockjaw because of the way it kills: the muscles, especially around the mouth, become rigid and the patient dies of suffocation. A toxin (poison) produced by the tetanus bacterium, which lives in the soil and enters the body through "dirty wounds," attacks the nerve cells in the spinal cord that control muscle activity. The first symptoms appear between two days and two weeks later. Most people are inoculated against tetanus, so the disease is extremely rare, striking only about 100 people in the United States each year. However, even with treatment the fatality rate is 40 percent. Booster shots administered every ten years provide complete protection against the bacterium; however, if you are not sure that you have been inoculated and you step on a thorn or a nail or are bitten by a squirrel, you should receive a tetanus shot immediately.

There's a fair amount of information contained in that paragraph, most of which is important to understanding how dangerous tetanus can be and how easy it is to prevent. Begin remembering this information by creating a **cue** for tetanus: **tennis nuts** should do the trick. But the image "tennis nuts" alone may not be sufficiently strong, because there's no semantic connection between "tennis nuts" and "tetanus," only a phonetic link. You want the **tennis nuts** to signal tetanus loud and clear in your mind. See the tennis nuts withering in pain on the court because they've stepped on rusty nails; as gruesome as the scene may be, see them screaming as they try to pull the nails out of their feet. By reinforcing this cue, you've also learned how tetanus is acquired.

To enhance your memory further, see the nails—very long nails—sticking right into a nerve; there's a drop of poison on the tip of the nail. Visualize either a drop of liquid you know is a poison or see **posted sun** on the point of the nail. Also on the head of the nail is a **bat ear** (bacteria) from which the poison is dripping. Now in some of these tennis nuts there's a **music station** (immunization) that prevents the **bat ear** from releasing the poison (perhaps because the music station is so loud—see everything vibrate from the sound. The tennis nuts who aren't listening to this music station die—see a rose in a purse (for 40 percent death rate) in their hands. One final piece of data: you must get an injection every ten years to be protected against tetanus. Add to this scene other tennis nuts waiting for a free court to play; they are being injected with a solution of toes (for 10 years).

There's another system you could have used to learn about tetanus: with the Top Ten list you could have created a cue for tetanus and then linked one bit of information about the disease to each number picture in the system. Use whichever you like better.

Cholera is almost unheard of in developed countries, but too common in the lesser-developed world. The disease is caused by bacteria that damage the intestinal lining and cause severe diarrhea, so that up to 4 *gallons* of fluid are lost a day. Cholera bacteria spread in unhygienic conditions and through contaminated fruits, vegetables, and water. The treatment involves replacing body fluids; antibiotics may be helpful.

Cholera can be remembered by a collar replacing a toilet seat; somebody's sitting on that toilet seat because he has diarrhea. (Unfortunately, there's no way to create vivid pictures to remember cholera without making unpleasant images.) At the same time, that person is drinking lots of water—visualize how the water passes right through his system.

To remember that cholera is a disease of the Third World (information possibly worth a point or two on the exam), make the bathroom a straw hut.

Finally, to recall that antibiotics are sometimes used in treating cholera, see an **ant** crawling on his **buttocks**. The ant stops the diarrhea.

11

Chemistry

Science—for some it's a love, for others a guaranteed C-minus. Part of the problem has to do with theory. Many scientific concepts are difficult (and many are simply poorly taught). But the bulk of the problem has to do with memorization: there's a fantastic amount of material to learn in any science course, especially chemistry. And it's very difficult to learn theory if you are struggling with the facts.

This chapter will alleviate that problem.

The Periodic Table of the Elements

If you know the structure of the periodic table, you know a great deal about how various elements behave. In this section we will focus on remembering elements and their atomic numbers. You'll be using surprise seeing, the link, mimicry, and the number system.

In the next hour you will learn the first fifty-six elements through the lanthanide series, which accounts for most of the elements in chemical reactions and all of the elements in organic molecules.

If you want to learn the atomic weights of particular elements (or if you need them), go ahead. To ensure that you don't confuse atomic weight with atomic number, link the image for the element to a scale (for weight), then link the scale to the atomic weight. In other words, create a cue for atomic weight.

Element	Symbol	Atomic Number
Hydrogen	H	1

Hydrogen, the first element on the periodic table, and the most common and lightest element in the universe, consists of a proton and electron. To remember that hydrogen is the first element on the periodic table, see the dirigible *Hindenburg*—filled with hydrogen, as you know. Notice how light it is. See it wearing a hat (the number 1 becomes hat, because 1 = t in the number system).

Helium	He	2

Helium is an excellent substitute for hydrogen to fill lighter-than-air craft. To remember that helium is the second element on the periodic table, see a **heel** with a **thumb** protruding out of it. The thumb is being pecked by a **hen.**

Lithium	Li	3

A **light thumb** (glowing, shining, whatever), being used to cut a **ham.** The act of cutting may also help you remember that lithium is a metal.

Beryllium   Be   4

A **bird** in a **room** (which is a place a bird would not want to be), stuck in somebody's **hair.**

Boron   B   5

Boring into a piece of **hail.**

Carbon   C   6

Carbon, sometimes called the element of life because its chemistry allows it to bind with so many different atoms in numerous ways, can be remembered in one of three ways: You can see a **carbon** filter, a **car bomb,** or something that's **carbonated**—whichever works best for you. If you use carbon filter, see it smothered with **ash** (to remember that carbon is the sixth element in the periodic table).

An interlude and example: Methane, CH_4, is a vital constituent of many organic molecules. To remember the formula, you could see a carbon filter as a table top supported by four dirigibles, like legs of a table. On top of the carbon table is a **moth** weather vane. It's very important to include a mimic for methane in your mnemonic because the only way to remember something is to have a cue. If, for example, you are asked the formula for methane, you may very well know the formula, CH_4, but have no way of *linking* it to methane. Similarly, if you see CH_4, you'll think of a carbon-filter table with dirigible legs, but you will have no clue that it stands for methane. So always include a cue.

Nitrogen   N   7

A **night Trojan** horse taking a **hike.** If what you are really interested in learning is that nitrogen is used for cooling materials to supercold temperatures, remember that "When it's **night again** it's very cold."

Oxygen   O   8

See an oxygen tank for underwater diving being filled with
O's—actually see those O's flowing into the tank. To prevent
the oxygen from leaking out, a hive is stuffed into the valve.
If you want to remember that liquid oxygen, LOX, is a space
rocket fuel, see the rocket as a hungry critter with an open
mouth, huge red lips, and a tongue that is licking those lips.
To satiate it, the rocket is fed lox on a bagel.

An interlude and example: H_2O_2 is the formula for hydrogen peroxide. You could remember the formula by thinking
"Ho-Ho, they're not going to peroxide my hair, too." Sound
can be a practical mnemonic for chemistry. Another mnemonic involves creating a mental picture of two dirigibles
being filled with O's from two different pumps. That image
has to be linked to peroxide: see the dirigibles carrying a **pear**
and **ox** on the out**side**.

Fluorine   F   9

Flour in **wine**, which is absurd; just as absurd is to use a
hoop to taste that wine.

Neon   Ne   10

See the gas in a neon light leaking out through a severe
crack. Hear it going *psss,* feel the pressure as you put your
hand to the broken part of the lamp; taste it, too—it tastes
cold. The scene is taking place in the capital of neon, Las
Vegas; someone thinks of using **dice** to fill the crack.
An alternative image involves a **knee on** something.

An interlude and example: Neon is an inert gas; it doesn't
react with anything. To remember that fact, envision someone trying to get a **knee on** a leg but not succeeding. It just
won't react the right way.

Sodium   Na   11

A **soda** tastes **yum** to a **tot**. Or see a **soda** with a **yam** in it
being drunk by a tot.

Magnesium   Mg   12

A **magnet easing** into **tin**.

Aluminum   Al   13

Aluminum foil wrapped around a **dome**.

Silicon   Si   14

A window**sill** with a **convict** on it (or a silly convict) with a gigantic **tear** coming out of his eye.

Phosphorus   P   15

There are two ways to turn phosphorus into a memorable image. First, you could fiddle with its application, as we did with carbon, and envision something that glows in the dark, is phosphorescent. Another option is to do what we are doing with most of the elements: substitute a memorable picture for the sound of the word "phosphorus." "A **fossil for us**," they exclaimed. "And it's a **tail!**"

Sulfur   S   16

A **surfer** surfing on a **dish**.

Chlorine   Cl   17

See **chlorine** dumped into a pool in excess. Or see someone **clawing** a **tack**.

An interlude and example: If you want to remember that NaCl, sodium chloride, is salt, see someone **clawing** to get that **yam** out of the **soda**. It doesn't work, so they sprinkle salt on it.

Argon   Ar   18

An **organ** so covered with **toffee** that it can't play a note.

Potassium   K   19

A **possum** eating *from* a **tub,** or a **pot** with **ash** in it. Should you want to remember the atomic weight of potassium,

39.102, think of this: He's a fat little possum, weighing 39 pounds, and the reason he's in the tub is because he has a fever of 102.

| Calcium | Ca | 20 |

Use a bone to represent calcium. It will work better than anything you could substitute for the sound, calcium. See a bone piercing through someone's **nose.**

| Scandium | Sc | 21 |

A **sandy gym** covered with a **net.**

| Titanium | Ti | 22 |

The *Titanic*—and covering the deck is a gigantic **nun.**

| Vanadium | V | 23 |

A weather **vane** on top of a **dome**; on top of the vane is a **gnome.**

| Chromium | Cr | 24 |

"**Chrome** is nowhere **near,**" said the explorer.

| Manganese | Mn | 25 |

A **magnified easel** with a **nail** driven through it.

| Iron | Fe | 26 |

A **tire** or fireplace **iron** piercing a dish.

An interlude and example: There's a chemistry joke that goes like this: What is this?

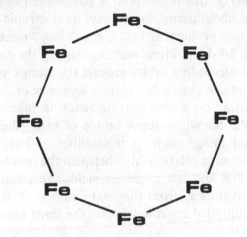

Answer: A Ferris wheel.

It's not a bad joke as far as chemistry jokes go, and it has the advantage of helping you remember that the symbol for iron is Fe.

| Cobalt | Co | 27 |

A **coal ball** being kicked by a **Nike** sneaker.

| Nickel | Ni | 28 |

A **nickel** that is pierced by a **knife**.

| Copper | Cu | 29 |

Copper wire wrapped around a **knob**.

| Zinc | Zn | 30 |

A zinc **Slinky** covered with **moss**.

| Gallium | Ga | 31 |

A **gale** wind swirling about **gum**; the gum lands on **mud**— quite a sticky mess.

Germanium   Ge   32

Geraniums on the **moon**. And if you wanted to learn some other things about germanium—say, its electronic configuration—that's no problem either. Germanium's electronic configuration is 2-8-18-4. These numbers signify the pairs of electrons in the succeeding orbits around the atom's nucleus. So, 2-8-18-4: you can certainly create a sequence of images such as a **hen** sitting on a **hive** getting ready to take a **dive** into some **roe**. Put the whole scene on top of an eggshell, or some other orbital image such as a satellite. Alternatively, you might notice some relationships between the numbers: Multiplying the first and last numbers yields the second number, which is 1 digit away from the next number. Or the first two numbers multiplied together equals the third number minus the last digit.

Arsenic   As   33

An **ass's neck** covered with **M & M's**.

Selenium   Se   34

A **sail** hoisted on **mums** (if you're not terrific with flowers, choose **mom** instead of mums). The mums are sailing through a **moor**.

Bromine   Br   35

A **broke mine**—there's a **mule** wandering through the mine.

Krypton   Kr   36

The planet Krypton, or a **crypt on** a **ham** covered with **ash**.

Rubidium   Rb   37

A **ruby yam** attached to a **mike**. (When you see mike in your mind, you'll know the image you've conjured means mike and *not* microphone, because you already have the knowledge that atomic numbers are two, at most three, digits; microphone would yield a very heavy element indeed.)

Strontium   Sr   38

A **strand** hanging off a **yam**; the yam is cool, so it's covered with a **muff.**

Yttrium   Y   39

Bit a **yam**, then covered it with a **robe.**

Zirconium   Zr   40

Make a picture of those fake **zirconium** jewels; in your image the jewelry should be a cheap and tinsel-looking as possible. There's a **rose** growing out of the jewelry.

Niobium   Nb   41

A **noisy room** with a **rat** running around.

Molybdenum   Mo   42

A **moldy yam** on an **iron.**

Technetium   Tc   43

A **tack** in a **neck** being shoved in by a **ram.**

Ruthenium   Ru   44

A **root yam** is very **rare.**

Rhodium   Rh   45

Imagine a **rhododendron** that's growing out of a **rail.**

Palladium   Pd   46

A **palace** of **yams**—a **rich** place.

Silver   Ag   47

Various silver items can be conjured for silver—a silver bullet, a silver tea set, a silver necklace. But whichever you choose, make certain that the image is memorable. A simple silver tea set *won't* be memorable, but a tea set that defies gravity and stays in place against the side of a wall (and holds tea that way) will be remembered. See a **rock** in that silver tea set.

Cadmium	Cd	48

A golf **caddy** with a hair and a hoof.

Indium	In	49

An **Indian** eating a **yam** and a **rib**.

Tin	Sn	50

A **tin** can filled with **laws**.

Antimony	Sb	51

Anti-money (create a picture that reminds you of anti-money) that is also a **light**.

Tellurium	Te	52

A **teller** under **delirium** (or a **tailor** with a **yam** for a head) being attacked by a **lion**.

Iodine	I	53

Imagine putting lots—a tremendous amount—of iodine on a cut. That shouldn't be too difficult to envision—or feel. The only way to relieve the suffering is to rub the wound against a **lamb**.

Xenon	Xe	54

Another noble gas; envision a **seat on** a **lyre**.

Cesium	Cs	55

Seizing a **yam** that is attached to a **lily**.

Barium	Ba	56

Barium is the liquid that people who are having X rays of their gastrointestinal tract drink. It's pretty foul stuff, and can create more than a simple queasy stomach. If you want to remember that use for barium think of **Barry** Manilow. Connect Barry Manilow to a **leash**.

You're on your own for the rest of the elements.

Organic Chemistry

Of course, the periodic table of the elements doesn't encompass everything you'll need to know in chemistry (though it is impressive in a pinch). Organic chemistry, physical chemistry, synthetic chemistry, molecular orbital chemistry, spectroscopy—all involve memorizing vast amounts of information. These subjects also involve learning theory and application, but having a vast store of knowledge at your fingertips will make learning theory and applying the theory —especially during exams—a great deal easier.

Let's take a look at some material you'll need to know for organic chemistry.

Electron orbitals and atomic electronic configurations are among the first things you have to tackle in any organic chem class, so let's examine them. You've probably encountered a phenomenon called the Pauli exclusion principle, which mandates that only two electrons can occupy an atomic orbital and these two electrons must have opposite spins. With that in mind, here are the orbital configurations for the first nine elements:

H	$1s$
He	$1s^2$
Li	$1s^2 2s$
Be	$1s^2 2s^2$
B	$1s^2 2s^2 2p$
C	$1s^2 2s^2 2p_x 2p_y$
N	$1s^2 2s^2 2p_x 2p_y 2p_z$

O $1s^22s^22p^2_xp2_y2p_z$
F $1s^22s^22p^2_x2p^2_y2p_z$

Normally, one's initial reaction to confronting a chart like this would be "Aghh!," which is an understandable reaction. But there's no need for panic, just as there's no need to understand what these orbitals are all about in order to memorize them. However, it's worth repeating here that *the more you do understand about what you are trying to memorize, the easier memorization becomes.* Knowing how an equation or definition is applied makes it easier to visualize that information, and thus create a strong mnemonic. The first thing we should look for is patterns. As you can see, every element (except for hydrogen) occupies the $1s^2$ orbital; because hydrogen has only one electron, it only has one electron to fill its orbital. The superscript ^{2} means two electrons; no superscript means only one electron in a particular orbital. Because every element occupies the 1s orbital, we can ignore that for the purposes of memorization, and concentrate on the significant information. Significant information means information that has to be memorized.

The best way to go about memorizing this is to assign each of the orbitals an image:

2s   becomes   Apartment 2s
$2p_x$ becomes   Duplex apartment
$2p_y$ becomes   penny
$2p_z$ becomes   Pez candy

As for the superscript ^{2}, which represents two electrons in an orbital, make a sharp image of a pair of electrons walking hand in hand.

Now that you have the components of this mnemonic, all that's left to do is link and assemble them into a memorable picture. Let's do that for carbon: Envision Apartment 2s with a very affectionate couple of electrons living inside. Dress the electrons—clothe them and give them male and female characteristics. Imagine them kissing as they wander from one level of their duplex to another. As they walk upstairs, pennies are pouring out of the pocket of the electrons. That gives you the orbitals. All that remains is to connect this image to carbon: Imagine that their entire apartment is **carbon**ated.

Free Radicals

Free radicals are unpaired electrons; electrons by themselves have a negative charge.

One common free radical reaction is the chlorination of sulfuryl chloride:

$$R\text{-}H + SO_2CL_2 \xrightarrow[\substack{\text{light or} \\ H_2O_2 \text{ (peroxide)}}]{40°\text{--}80°\ C} R\text{-}Cl + SO_2 + HCl$$

This kind of equation becomes easier to learn once you know some of the theory behind it, but if you're simply interested in passing an exam or impressing your friends, you don't need to know the theory.

R- stands for any group of carbon atoms. So in place of **R**-envision a charcoal barbecue. Attach the barbecue to a dirigible, the symbol for hydrogen. The dirigible could be baking on the barbecue, which would likely cause some incredible *reaction*. Before we connect the dirigible to SO_2Cl_2 in some meaningful way, we have to convert SO_2Cl_2 into a memorizable notion. The phrase **"so to clean"** works as a mnemonic—SO_2 becomes "so 2," and Cl becomes "**clean.**" **So to clean a dirigible on a barbecue** is the mnemonic for the first part of the reaction (the reagents). When these two chemicals come into contact with light or peroxide (H_2O_2), there's a reaction. To represent this stage of the reaction, the yields, use the mnemonic for $=$ that we found helpful in the math chapter—a seesaw. Place the dirigible apparatus on one side of the seesaw. In the middle, put a brilliantly shining **light** bulb, or an amorphous glowing light (as if from a grade-B science fiction movie), *and* a bucket of **peroxide**. If you can't create a picture for peroxide, use mimicry and put a **pear** wearing socks on its side. Another alternative for peroxide is to use the chemical formula H_2O_2, which for our purposes is water (H_2O) $\times$ 2—two drops of water, standing on the seesaw, hand in hand.

Let's not forget the temperature range necessary for this reaction, either, 40–80 degrees centigrade. Balance a thermometer—which stands for temperature in all mnemonic systems for chemical reactions—on the seesaw. At one end of the thermometer there's a rose, on the other a vase. Centigrade is assumed.

On the other side of the seesaw place a barbecue with **chlorine,** the kind that gets dumped in a pool, on it. In addition to the barbecuing chlorine there are 2 sodas (soda is the mnemonic for SO) and HCl. HCl is one of those frequently occurring chemicals, so it's useful to create a once-and-for-all mnemonic for it: a dirigible in a heavily chlorinated swimming pool. HCl, hydrogen chloride, is a liquid, so the swimming pool mnemonic is even more practical.

The Preparation of Epoxides by Oxidation of Ethylene

A couple of other reactions are worth looking at. First, the preparation of epoxides by oxidation of ethylene (CH_2CH_2) by oxygen on a silver catalyst:

$$2CH_2 = CH_2 + O_2 \xrightarrow[\text{Ag catalyst}]{260°-290° \text{ C}} 2CH_2-CH_2 \diagdown \diagup O$$

There's a fair amount of information here that needs to be mastered; but memorizing this equation is easier and more permanent if you make pictures out of it than it would be by rote memorization.

The first part of our task involves turning two ethylene molecules, $CH_2 = CH_2$, into something memorable. Imagine the molecule as a bridge: the 2 is the major support that goes into the earth, the **CH**'s are the turrets, and the =, of course, is the bridge's span. Throughout this chapter we've been creating permanent mnemonics for chemical symbols; from now on ethylele is a bridge. Link bridge to ethylene by imagining the **Eiffel** Tower leaning against a bridge.

Oxygen also needs a symbol. You could use the image we developed for atomic oxygen, O, for molecular oxygen, O_2—O's coming out of an oxygen tank. You don't have to worry about confusing molecular and atomic oxygen; if you've gotten this far in chemistry, you'll know that individual oxygen atoms rarely occur in chemical reactions. So, someone is spraying the bridge with **O**'s, covering the bridge, which, by the way, happens to be made out of **silver**, the catalyst. The temperature is important for the reaction, too. You might want to remember that it occurs at a high temperature and simply imagine the silver bridge glowing bright red, or you might want to recall the approximate temperature, which should be sufficient, 270 degrees C. Place a couple of *hot*—glowing red—**nukes** on one side of the bridge. On the other side of the bridge will be the product of the reaction, the epoxide ethylene oxide, $2CH_2 - CH_2$.

$$\begin{array}{ccc} & \diagdown & \diagup \\ & & O \end{array}$$

How to remember this compound, *and* its structure? Well, on the other side of the bridge, someone is building another bridge. They haven't gotten very far: to date, just the supports have been completed (CH_2 is forever a bridge support), as well as half the span. To hold the span in place while the bridge is being completed, there's a giant balloon lifting the apparatus. You can figure out two ethylene oxide molecules will be created in this equation by counting the number of carbon atoms on the left side of the equation and remembering the principle that matter cannot be destroyed or created in chemical reactions, or you can put two bridges under construction and remember the information visually.

Friedel-Crafts Alkylation

A reaction popular for exams in organic chemistry is called the Friedel-Crafts alkylation and it goes like this:

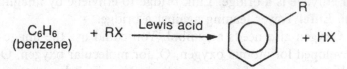

$$C_6H_6 \text{ (benzene)} + RX \xrightarrow{\text{Lewis acid}} \text{(benzene ring with R)} + HX$$

For benzene, imagine a snake in a circle eating its tail. The snake forms a ring and resembles the benzene. (This mnemonic has historical significance; benzene's discoverer envisioned its structure by dreaming about a benzene molecule as a snake catching its tail.)

The snake is taking a prescription medication, an **RX**, as one might expect for a snake in its condition. It has to take it quickly because there's a **loose acid**. Well, the prescription and the loose acid affect the snake in unforeseen ways: a barbecue is now growing out of the snake's side. Obviously, there's a **hex** on the snake.

To remember that this is something called the **Friedel-Crafts** alkylation (alkylation is less important to know than Friedel-Crafts) imagine **fried crafts** in that barbecue.

Create Your Own Mnemonic Lists

This is probably a good time for you to develop your own list of chemistry mnemonics. You have already covered many of the building blocks of chemical equations and examined the mnemonic foundations that provide a way to create whatever memory system you need for chemistry. However, if you continue to study chemistry you will need more symbols for chemicals, definitions, and structures. It's frequently easier to make a set of mnemonic building blocks—like the periodic table of the elements—than to create a new set of memory pictures each time you have something to remember.

12

Physics and Geology

Learning physics and other hard sciences such as geology and electromagnetism is about 75 percent memorization and 25 percent panic. This chapter, by solving the 75 percent problem, will also take care of the panic.

The examples in this chapter, which come from popular college physics textbooks, will accomplish three objectives. First, they will teach you some physics, geology, and electromagnetism, always a good thing if you're studying the subject. Second, the examples provide specific mnemonics that apply to these subjects. Third, the examples will offer you strategies for memorizing other information you'll encounter later.

So without further delay let's jump into developing memory techniques for physics.

Average Velocity

The expression for **average velocity** is

$\bar{v} = \dfrac{L}{T}$, where v is average velocity, L is length, and T is time.

For the velocity mnemonic, it's good to imagine an Austin-Martin, Porsche, or some other very fine sports car. Select whichever you want and make that sports car the symbol for velocity from now on.

For length, choose a tie. Why a tie? Well, an L sort of looks like a tie, and as every tie tier knows, trying to get the tie's length adjusted correctly can be quite a chore.

For time, a grandfather clock will do.

There's a brilliant red Porsche on one end of a seesaw, revving its engine, ready to head toward the other end of the seesaw at which there's a tie trying to cut a grandfather clock in half with a knife (remember from the mathematics chapter that this is the mnemonic for division). Actually see a tie with little arms and legs, kind of like a Gumby image.

Power, Work, and Time

Another formula: power equals the time rate at which work is done:

$$P = \frac{W}{t}$$

We'll need a symbol for P, or power. Plenty of possibilities come to mind: 1) A mighty P with human qualities and plenty of muscles; 2) a stick of dynamite; 3) a powerful engine; 4) a king.

Work is easy to envision: A stack of physics textbooks.

The equation: an engine on one side of the railroad tracks;

on the other side is a stack of physics textbooks precariously balanced on top of a grandfather clock. It's actually the engine, through its power, that is keeping the books in place.

Work and Force

More in the formula department:

$W = FD \cos\theta$ where F is force and D is distance.

For F, force, use the mnemonic **force** field—a science fiction concept, but a vivid image nonetheless. For D, distance, there are many possible images you can create; the one I prefer is a discus thrower, who of course will try to hurl the discus as great a distance as it can travel.

See a stack of physics textbooks piled on one end of a seesaw. Weighing down the other end of the seesaw is a discus thrower trying to hurl the discus through a force field. He is trying to accomplish this many **times** (for force times distance). You'll recall from the mathematics chapter that cosine can be represented by $ (cost sounds a bit like cosine). There are several bags of $s awaiting the discus thrower if he can penetrate the force field; there are bags of eggs with belts (theta) for him if he fails.

Torque

Physics is no good without definitions, so here's the definition of torque (moment of force). Torque describes rotational motion around an axis that accompanies the application of force. Torque, then, is product of force times lever arm, (which is the perpendicular distance from the axis to the line of action of the force). For torque, a practical mnemonic would be a **torch.** Place the torch on one side of a seesaw. On the other side you want to create an image for force times lever arm. Force already has a mnemonic—force field—but lever arm doesn't. You could either envision an image that relates to the sound "lever arm," or one that reminds you of lever arm's meaning. Obviously, if your mnemonic for lever arm encompasses the term's definition, your overall mne-

monic will contain a more complete definition of torque. But
if you decide that you don't need to have all that information
immediately available, just memorize the minimal amount of
information. Use the rule of thumb we've applied for other
subjects: *Memorize the least amount of information you have
to know.* Lever arm lends itself well to several mnemonic
devices. The simplest is to see a human arm attached to a
lever. The arm tries numerous **times** to penetrate the force
field.

And that's all you need to know for the definition of
torque.

Mechanics and Equilibrium

Let's look at a couple more definitions while we're exploring this subject. In mechanics, the first condition of equilibrium is that **the vector sum of all forces acting upon a body
must equal zero**.

As usual, the first step is to break this definition into its
component parts:

First condition A pen (the image for 1 in our list of 1–10)
   sticking out of a bottle of hair conditioner.
Equilibrium An aquarium (for fish to survive in the aquar-
   ium, water, temperature, purity, salinity all must be in
   equilibrium). Notice, too, that there is some correspon-
   dence of sound between the two.
Vector sum Vectors are represented by arrows, so the mne-
   monic for vector sum can be a great many arrows piled on
   top of one another—that is, added together.
Forces Force fields
Acting on Acting
Body A sleeping body
Equal Seesaw or railroad tracks
Zero Hose

Definitions are notoriously difficult to memorize, because
getting them correct means pursuing elusive verbatim memo-

rization. However, locating the important thoughts in the definition, listing them, and linking these images together is the way to ensure that you will remember the precise definition and not just the general idea.

Putting the first condition of equilibrium together: Conjure an image of a pen sticking out of a bottle of hair conditioner that is (for some strange reason having to do with physics, no doubt) floating in an aquarium (the fish don't mind). Inside the aquarium is a large collection of arrows—living arrows that are acting (perhaps a scene out of *Hamlet)* on top of a body, also in the aquarium. By now you should be used to the seesaw image for equals, but if you are also tired of it, substitute railroad tracks. (You are always free to create your own mnemonic for any concept in this book.) On the other side of the railroad tracks (I guess the aquarium is a kind of miniature Atlantis) is simply a hose—or a giant zero.

The second condition of equilibrium says that for coplanar forces acting on a body, the sum of all torques taken around any axis perpendicular to the plane of the forces must equal zero.

If you are having trouble memorizing physics formulas, don't write the formulas over and over again. Instead draw a picture of the image you want to use as that formula's mnemonic. Remembering the picture is easier than remembering the formula, and the clearer the image becomes in your mind's eye, the faster and more secure your memory will be. Pictures are always easier to remember than words and especially easier to remember than formulas.

Again, let's break the definition into its key ideas.

Second condition A swan
Equilibrium Aquarium
Coplanar force A plane bouncing off a force field
Acting Acting
Body A sleeping (or, yes, dead) body
Sum An adding machine
Zero Hose

An overall mnemonic shouldn't be too difficult to come by. Start by seeing a swan in a bottle of hair conditioner inside an aquarium. That image, representing **second condition**, will be your cue.

A plane is trying to land in the aquarium but can't because the aquarium is surrounded by a force field. Instead the plane chooses to pursue an acting career and starts by doing a routine on top of a dead **body** (not so funny; so much for the plane's career). The plane is holding an adding machine in one arm (wing) and a torch in the other arm (wing).

Velocity

Back to formulas for a bit. Velocity is defined as

$v = \int a \, dt$, the integral of instantaneous acceleration with respect to time.

We'll need a mnemonic for instantaneous acceleration. A space rocket taking off will suffice. Again, place the Porsche on one side of a seesaw. On the other, see Superman (the mnemonic for integral) standing next to a rocket blasting off (only Superman could). The rocket is carrying into space a grandfather clock attached to the outside, instead of the Space Shuttle.

An important formula for momentum (the product of mass times velocity (mv) is

$$F = m \frac{dv}{dt} = ma \quad \text{where m (mass) is a constant.}$$

The only symbol we don't yet have a mnemonic for is m, or mass. As usual, there are several possibilities open to us: The planet Earth, a very **mass**ive object, or a mass of people saying mass—my preference.

Envision a balance scale with three instead of two platters to hold objects to be weighed. Surround the first platter with a force field. In the other outside platter place a mass of people saying mass in a rocket that is blasting off. In the middle platter put water running through a pipe (the image for derivative with respect to x—see the chapter on mathematics) and notice that the water spills out of the pipe off the scale and onto the mass of people saying Mass. This happens many times. The mass of mass sayers gets upset so they take off in a Porsche.

Hydrostatic Pressure

Hydrostatic pressure (fluid pressure) is represented by the formula:

$$p = \frac{\Delta F}{\Delta A} \text{ as } \Delta A \longrightarrow 0$$

Force, F, acting on a unit area, A, is another way of saying that pressure, p, exists.

Three new symbols are introduced here, p for pressure, A for unit area, and Δ for change. Before putting a grand mnemonic together, let's create mini-mnemonics for these three concepts. For pressure, use a winepress, a headache commercial in which someone's head is depicted suffering from tremendous pressure, an egg being crushed in someone's hand, or a printing **press**. I like the headache commercial mnemonic, but whichever you select, be consistent. It's important to let only one image represent any given concept. For unit area, make your mnemonic **unlit acre**. For Δ, pronounced delta, which is simply the symbol for change, you have the option of selecting a mnemonic that reminds you directly of "change" or of "delta." I prefer to use a mnemonic that corresponds to "delta" rather than "change" because when I see the formula I see and think delta, and only later think that it means change. (If you want to use change, pocket **change** would work as a mnemonic.) For Δ, the Great Pyramids are a terrific image, but if your mind struggles with the Pyramids, then a billiard bracket or any other traditionally triangular object will suffice. To put it all together:

See this person with a tremendous pressure headache and a translucent head, so that you can see the internal pressure, sitting on a seesaw. On the other side of the seesaw is a Great Pyramid resting against an equally great force field. The one Pyramid is balanced—precariously; see it teetering—on top of another Great Pyramid which is in a one-acre unlit field. See the darkened lamps around the field, make a mental note that the field *ought to* be lit. As for the part of the equation $\Delta A \longrightarrow O$, you could try to create an image that relates to the phrase "delta A as it approaches O," but there's a more straightforward way of doing this. See an arrow being fired from the acre at an O; as vividly as you can, see the arrow pierce the center of the O, a hose.

GEOLOGY

Learning geology isn't too different from learning physics or even economics. Although the subject matter is quite different, the educational principles on which geology courses are based are almost identical to the other subjects we've been exploring in this book: Most of what you need to know in your geology course—especially for exams and answering questions in class—is memorization, and the more facts you have at your disposal the easier it will be to learn geological theories and to apply those theories. Geologists—and geology students—must have a great deal of information at their fingertips.

Facts about Earth

Let's begin with some basic information about Earth, our home planet.

Diameter	7,918 miles
Mean distance from the sun	92.9 million miles

Circumference around the equator	24,900 miles
Mass	6,600 quintillion (6,600,000,000,000,000,000) tons
Axis of inclination	23.5 degrees
Height of tallest mountain	over 29,000 feet (Everest)
Greatest known depth of the ocean	36,560 feet

The diameter of the Earth can be represented by imaging the Earth held **captive** by a giant ruler through its middle. The Earth struggles to get free, but it is a captive and cannot.

The distance from the sun can be remembered by seeing a **pinup** (for 92.9) stretching between Earth and the sun. Your common sense will alert you that the 92.9 is million, not thousands or billion.

The number 24,900, Earth's circumference, also has a straightforward numerical representation: See **troops** baring their ass standing around the Earth's equator.

Earth's mass is a bit more unusual a project. The number 6,600 becomes **cha-cha saws**; funny thing to see, saws doing the cha-cha. (Again, your intuition will help you organize the information; common sense tells you that 66 comes before 00, otherwise the number wouldn't make any sense.) But what about quintillion? Making a mnemonic exclusively out of seventeen s's (s = 0) would be interesting, and would probably create the world's most difficult tongue twister. Better to devise a mnemonic for quintillion. How about a **quilt** with what seems like a quintillion number of patches on it? Put the cha-chaing saws on top of the quilt, and stuff the whole thing inside the Earth.

Axis of inclination, 23.5, becomes a **gnome** (remember, silent letters are ignored in the number system) hail. See a gnome throwing hail at the Earth and this causes the Earth to tilt on its axis. You may want to include **axis** as the cue word for this piece of information because you may want "axis" to trigger your memory of the angle at which the Earth is tilted. If so, see the gnome sitting on a car axis. It's uncomfortable; the gnome is grumbling to himself, and the more uncomfortable he becomes the harder he hurls those hailstones at the earth.

I'll leave the height of the tallest mountain and ocean depth to you.

The Atmosphere

The Earth is divided into three major geologic divisions: the lithosphere (the Earth's crust and upper mantle); the hydrosphere (composed mostly of water—that is, the ocean basins), which also contains absorbed air and particles of rock; and the atmosphere (a sphere of air that also contains absorbed water and small amounts of rock in the form of dust).

Lithosphere   Envision a **spherical** lithograph composed of rock, bread **crust,** and **mantles** from people's homes.

Hydrosphere   Envision a **spherical** hydroplane traveling through the oceans

Atmosphere   As mentioned several times in *The Student's Memory Book,* don't bother devising mnemonics for information you already know.

Earthquakes

Geology is, if nothing else, a spectacular science. One of the most spectacular—and destructive—geological events is the earthquake. Earthquakes are classified into three types, according to the depth of the quake. Shallow quakes, the most common, occur within 60 kilometers of the surface, and most shallow quakes begin less than 7 km down. Intermediate quakes originate from 70 to 300 km below the surface. Deep quakes begin lower than 300 km, down to a depth of 720 kilometers. The energy radiated by an earthquake travels in waves through rock, which takes on the property of an elastic body. As these waves move they are affected by diffraction, refraction, reflections, and dispersion; the rocks vibrate and move and the waves become quite complex.

There are three types of earthquake waves. P waves are also called primary, compressional, or longitudinal waves. The P wave is also a fast-body wave that journeys rapidly through the earth's interior. It is transmitted by alternating expansion and compression of the volume of rock and travels in a direct path; P waves can travel through solid, liquid, or gas. P waves travel at between 6.0 to 11.3 kilometers per second. The P wave is the first to arrive at a seismograph station.

S waves are also called secondary, shear, or transverse waves; it is a slower body wave than the P wave. It also travels through the Earth's interior, and arrives second at a seismograph station. S waves are transmitted by vibrations at right angles to the path the wave travels in the rock. (Similar to light waves, while P waves are more like sound waves.) S waves cannot go through liquids. They move at between 3.5 and 7.3 kps.

L waves are also known as long or surface waves. These slow, undulating waves travel just beneath the surface of the Earth. There are two kinds of L waves: "Love waves" move in uniform solids and "Raleigh waves" move through nonuniform solids. Although slow, these waves carry considerable energy and can move around the Earth more than once. The wave travels at about 3.5 kps.

Knowing the difference between these waves is crucial to understanding how they work. So let's develop some mnemonics for them. Once again, we need a cue to link all this information to. An aquarium filled not with fish, but with waves, is a good mnemonic filer; visualize the aquarium's waves becoming agitated. Reach into the tank and grab a P wave; you'll know you've got a P wave because it has a **long tide** (longitudinal) and it's **compressed**. Pay particular attention to how compressed the wave is and how it uncompresses after you pull it out of the water. As soon as you grab the wave, it leaps from your hand, dashes to a globe across the room, and goes directly to the center of the globe, which happens to be made of solid, gas, and liquid. The globe once was an inflatable beach ball and got filled with water and sand. There are other beach-related items stuffed in the beach-ball globe as well; the wave picks them up as it bounces along the globe's interior. These include a **compress** that **expands** as the wave hits it. (Alternatively, you could visualize rock inside the globe actually expanding and compressing, as it does when exposed to a P wave.) To learn its velocity, see the P wave wiggling along some **ash**, but only in the **daytime**. (Again, your intuition will tell you where to place the decimal point, but if you are worried about that, see the wave eating a **date** removing the pit—which looks like a period—then eating a **ham**.)

S waves are also swimming around the aquarium. Go ahead, grab one; they're slower than the P wave so they will be easier to catch. In fact, the S waves are so uncomfortable in liquid that they can't move through it. Cut the wave with a **shear** to prevent it from going through the **transverse** down the block. One of the most significant differences between P and S waves is that the latter are transmitted at right angles to the path that the wave travels in the rock. Instead of moving directly ahead, trying to escape in that direction as the P wave did, the S wave levitates upward, at a *right angle* to the direction you would expect it to take. The last piece of information we have to learn about S waves is how fast they move: Envision that one struggling to get past a **mole** that's blocking their path, but since it can't move through liquid, the only way for the S wave to get across is to use a **comb** as a bridge.

L waves: Notice that they are far, far **longer** than any of the other waves in the tank; they like to travel along the **surface** of the aquarium. There are two kinds of L waves in the aquarium. The Love waves are very cozy among themselves; the Raleigh waves are smoking Raleighs—that's how you tell the difference. The Love waves are also wearing **uniforms** though their clothing is made of **solids**; the Raleigh waves are not wearing uniforms, but are also wearing solids. The L waves are not moving very fast because they are eating a meal.

PART THREE

Putting It All Together

13

Mnemonics in a Nutshell

In the first few chapters of *The Student's Memory Book* you learned the theory, as well as the basic techniques for remembering information: surprise seeing, the link, organization, the Top Ten system, the cue, rhyme, and remembering numbers were among them. In the book's later chapters you practiced and refined these techniques. You also adapted them to particular subjects *and* developed variants to the basic methods such as the Room system, map grids, and mnemonics for the chemistry and physics.

Because it's best to learn about how to use these techniques through actual applications than simply through theory, *The Student's Memory Book* was designed to teach by example. In

some cases you learned some memory methods before knowing that these techniques had a distinct name. Now you know
how to remember everything. This chapter puts all the mnemonics together in one place.

SKILLS THAT ARE NECESSARY FOR EVERY MNEMONIC TECHNIQUE

1. *Pay attention.* You must concentrate on what you want
to remember. There is no such thing as learning through
osmosis. Study only when you are able to focus. Think about
what you are doing.

2. *You have to want to learn the material.* People remember
only the information they have a desire to retain. This is a
natural biological property of human beings; if we remembered every image and fact we encountered, our brains would
quickly become cluttered. Both your conscious and subconscious minds have to crave the material—if not out of love,
then out of fear of failure.

3. *Divide what you want to learn into manageable chunks*
and eliminate what you don't need to learn. Perform triage
on your courses. You will probably have more motivation if
there is less to learn. Aim your mnemonics at particular
goals. Don't try to learn a gigantic subject such as *Romeo
and Juliet* all at once; focus on the plot, then the characters,
then the setting, then the author's message, the symbolism,
and so forth.

4. *You have to structure the material so that you can actually recall it later.* The information must be organized and
tidied up so that you can find it among the other important
stuff in your brain, such as the key answers in Trivial Pursuit
and what you're going to do Saturday night. Organization
requires you to create a **cue** (which will be explained as a
separate mnemonic below) *and* an overall structure for the
information. Your mental filing cabinet must be organized or

you will never find anything in it. Look for patterns, similarities, differences, and analogies in the information.

5. *Study only when you are in a good frame of mind.* Depression and anxiety, for example, are enemies of memory, as are being tired or overexcited. You simply won't be able to learn when your psyche is out of balance. When you can't study, your time is better spent resting, going to a Marx Brothers movie, or exercising. Then try studying again.

6. *Use your imagination.* Your imagination is the cornerstone of your ability to memorize large amounts of information. This includes giving action to normally stationary objects and transforming them in ways that don't necessarily exist in nature. Always have your imagination in the **on** position. And trust your imagination! Most of the time, whatever image—mnemonic—enters your mind first is the best one.

7. *Use your senses.* The perceptions of the senses encompass many attributes: Feel things, see their color, their shape, texture, movement, what they smell like, whether they make a sound. Shake them and see if they rattle. Look at them and see if they reflect sunlight.

7. *Review.* Mnemonics is not magic. You will have to repeat the material you've just "memorized" if you want to make it a permanent feature of your memory. After you've created a mnemonic for something, go back a couple of minutes later and revive the image in your head. Then do that again in an hour or so. And then the next day for sure. Review is painless, especially with mnemonics, but absolutely essential.

8. *Have fun.* One of the differences between mnemonics and rote memorization is that memory techniques are fun. They involve making pictures, doing rhymes, creating stories. The more fun you have, the easier memorization becomes.

The Major Mnemonic Techniques

All the major mnemonic techniques require you to think visually. They all work because we remember pictures better than mere words. The operative word is *visualization*.

1. *Surprise seeing* is simply another way of saying seeing something in a memorable way. Frequently it involves turning an ordinary object into an object with extranormal characteristics. With surprise seeing *you must create images in your mind's eye. Surprise seeing is a visual technique; it requires conjuring bold, believable-to-you and detailed images of what you want to remember.* Surprise seeing works because the brain loves novelty, and hates habit and familiarity. You must surprise your mind, trick it into remembering what ordinarily would be a boring, forgettable image or idea. Usually the image that first pops into your head is the best one. For example, if you want to remember to buy a pizza on the way home from work, you shouldn't think "buy a pizza." Instead, imagine your friend turning *you* into a pizza if you forget one—see her smother you with tomato sauce, mushrooms, and cheese, and stick you in the oven.

2. *The Link, or Image Association* involves connecting two or more items you want to remember. Because linking is also visual, it means that you connect the pictures of these objects or ideas. In order for the link to be successful, the connections must be a) clearly seen in your mind's eye, b) actually touching, and c) as contextual as possible. Link things in a way that makes sense. For example, if you want to remember to buy an umbrella and a toaster on the way home, don't see the toaster resting on top of the umbrella. Connect the two by placing the umbrella on top of the toaster to keep the rain from falling into the slots (which could be calamitous). You can link as many items together as you want. Long lists of items can be made into a story.

The link is a way of organizing information so that you can recall it.

3. *The Cue* is in some ways the most important mnemonic technique. The cue, or prompt, is the connection between the information stored in our brains and the external request to recall that information. The cue makes you think "ah-ha" and then the information bubbles out. The cue breaks through the "tip of the tongue" problem. The cue must be *strongly* linked to the information you are learning. It is the most crucial mnemonic in the chain of information you create. An example: You want to remember who was the twenty-ninth President of the United States, Harding. Create a mnemonic for 29. **Knob** works fine. Substitute a concrete English phrase for Harding, such as **hard ring**. Convert hard ring to a solid picture—a hard ring. Link the two by placing the **hard ring** on the knob; the ring can't be removed from the knob. This image is all very well and good, because thinking 29 will lead you to knob, which will conjure the image hard ring. But you won't necessarily know that hard ring means Harding unless you create a cue that reminds you of **President**. See the hard ring on a door of the White House. White House is the cue. If, however, you were asked, "Who was the twenty-ninth President of the United States?" you would already know that President was involved, so knob would be the cue. The link between the cue and the rest of the information has to be dynamic or you will not remember it. Generally, the best cue is the first one that comes to your mind.

The cue is another aspect of organizing information.

4. *Mimicry* is used to remember concepts, foreign language vocabulary, names—anything that isn't a concrete image. Mimicry works by converting the abstract sounds into a clear picture, usually by first turning these sounds into an English word or phrase and then linking the picture with what you want to remember. Through this technique, any abstraction or idea can be turned into a clear image and remembered. For example, if you want to know the French word for ham, *jambon,* conjure the image of someone **jamming** a ham **bone** into their mouth. Substitute an English word or phrase for

the sounds and make a picture of it. The mimicry should have a) a phonetic resemblance between the sounds and the substituted words, and b) a semantic relationship.

Other Mnemonic Techniques

1. *The Top Ten system* creates a framework for remembering any list of up to ten items. It also works well for remembering remarks you hear during a lecture, or information presented in a chapter. Each number, 1 through 10, is assigned an image that looks like the shape of that number. To remember information, you link the data to be learned to that number.

1	is a	pen
2	is a	swan
3	is a	bird in flight
4	is a	sailboat
5	is a	hook
6	is a	golf club
7	is a	cliff
8	is a	snowman
9	is a	lollipop
10	is a	bat and ball

Frequently the number pictures in the Top Ten system serve as your cue. And, as always, the link between the number picture and what you want to know should be vivid.

2. *The Room system* is a variation of the Top Ten system. With this system you link things you want to remember to permanently fixed objects in your house or apartment. One thing to be remembered is visually attached to each item of furniture. Always "walk" through the same rooms in the same order, perhaps living room first, then kitchen, dining room, den, master bedroom, guest room, and basement. Always "walk" through the items in the rooms in the same order; clockwise from the door as you enter the room is best. Recalling information is easy because you simply visualize

the piece of furniture in your house and the image that's connected to that furniture—what you want to remember—pops into your head.

You can also assign numbers to each piece of furniture so that you can create permanent lists of information for information that lends itself to numerical lists, such as the Ten Commandments, the periodic table of the elements, or U.S. Presidents. For example, there may be eight pieces of furniture in your personal room #1, and ten in room #2. The second piece of furniture in room #2, the kitchen, is refrigerator. If you are trying to remember who the tenth President of the United States is you would link Tyler to refrigerator, because the refrigerator is the tenth piece of furniture in your personal Room system.

Everybody has his or her own personal Room system.

3. *The Rhyme List system.* The Top Ten system, the Room system and the Rhyme List system are all techniques for remembering lists of information, whether they are sections of a legal code, members of Congress, or types of plants. The Rhyme List system provides an alternative way of remembering 1 to 10 items:

> 1 is bun
> 2 is shoe
> 3 is tree
> 4 is door
> 5 is hive
> 6 is sticks
> 7 is heaven
> 8 is gate
> 9 is vine
> 10 is hen

You attach what you want to remember to the rhymed word. This system will allow you to remember numbers of limited length. For example, if you want to remember 349, envision a tree with a door in it and a vine growing around the door.

4. *The Major Number system* can turn digits of any length into memorable images. It works by assigning each digit, 1 to 0, a consonant sound. Vowels are then added to make words, and the words are turned into pictures. This system takes a little more practice than learning the other systems, but it is worth doing if you work with numbers. It becomes easier as you practice it. Some simple rules apply: Only consonants have numerical value. Only sounds are relevant; gh can sound like g (which is not represented in this system) or like f (which is 8). Double letters, like the 2 t's in the word letter, are treated as a single sound.

The sounds that represent consonants are as follows:

1	t,d
2	n
3	m
4	r
5	l
6	sh, ch
7	k, hard g (as in golf)
8	f,v,th
9	p,b
0	z,s

5. *Symbol Conversion* is the process of converting commonly used symbols into concrete images. This process is essential to being able to remember complex mathematical and scientific formulas. The mnemonic should have some phonetic connection to the symbol, should look like the symbol, or should remind you of the symbol. Some examples include $=$ as a seesaw; $\int$ (integral) as Superman; A, acceleration, as a Porsche; sin as sinning; and % as a purse.

6. *Chunking is an organizational technique* through which lengthy information is broken down into more manageable components. It is a way of preventing your mind from be-

coming overwhelmed, from being intimidated. Chunking is done all the time. Phone numbers are divided into a group of three digits followed by four digits; license plate numbers in the District of Columbia are divided into two sets of three digits. Unchunked information may be forgotten all at once; when you chunk information you have a better chance of remembering at least some of it.

7. *Making stories* is a variation of image association. Instead of merely linking images together, you can weave the pictures into a sequential tale. People tend to have a good memory for plots. This is a particularly useful technique for when you are trying to learn about the characters and plots of plays, novels, and poems, because these forms are already stories. But it also works for mathematics and history. Make the images in your stories vivid and the links between actions, characters, and objects as clear as possible. Keep your imagination open to detail.

8. *Acronyms* are terrific tools for remembering related information. Using acronyms as mnemonic devices involves making a word out of the first letter of each of the items you want to remember. Make a picture of that word and link it to a cue that will prompt you to remember the acronym. Using HOMES to remember the names of the Great Lakes is an example. And everyone remembers Roy G. Biv, who tells us the colors of the spectrum. (Red orange yellow green blue indigo violet.)

9. *Acronymic sentences take the first letter of each of the things you want to remember and turn them into words, which are then strung into sentences.* For example, to learn the order of the planets from the sun, the phrase "Meek violet extraterrestrials make just such unusual new pets." Make these phrases fun and you will remember them.

9. *Rhyme* is a potent, time-honored mnemonic technique. There are plenty of rhymes we learned as children and still remember today, such as:

> In fourteen hundred ninety-two,
> Columbus sailed the ocean blue.

When you can transform information into a rhyme, do so. Hear the cadence in the rhyme. In addition, make a picture of that rhyme to reinforce your memory.

10. *Finding faces* is a technique that is very helpful when learning history. It involves locating photographs or drawings of the people, places, and events you need to learn. Rather than conjure a fanciful image of that event, you actually find somebody else's image and use that as your mnemonic stepping-stone. Perhaps you want to remember certain things about Leonardo da Vinci's inventions. Begin by finding a picture of da Vinci and sketches of those inventions. Pay attention to the details in the images.

11. *Months* have their own, simple mnemonic system, which is covered in the chapter on history. (June equals Jewel and December is a Christmas tree, for example.) Months are the kind of information—a set of related information that is used over and over again—that lends itself well to creating separate mnemonics; this technique can be easily used for other, similar kinds of information. Develop the mnemonics as you need them.

12. The *Map system* enables you to locate objects on any map. It works by superimposing a chessboard-like grid on top of a map. Because each section of the grid you create can be represented by the intersection of points along the horizontal and vertical axes, you can quickly locate any point on the map below the grid. Along the horizontal axis are numbers; along the vertical axis, letters. Combine the letters and numbers to form words, so that each section of the grid can be identified by a unique word. The words, of course, become images through mnemonics.

13. *Sensible shortcuts* enable you to focus on the important components of what you're trying to memorize and are particularly helpful when it comes to memorizing long passages.

You don't have to memorize everything to remember everything. For example, when learning quotations: articles, punctuation, and words that are repeated often can be ignored. They will fall into place once you know the important parts.

What to Do When You Can't Remember

No memory technique is perfect because no mind is perfect. Everybody forgets and everybody makes mistakes. (Even the vaunted SAT exams contain errors.) So there will be times when you simply can't remember, when the information will be "on the tip of your tongue" despite mnemonics. When this happens there are steps you can take to recall the information.

The first step is to relax and, if you can, put the problem aside. Once you've posed a problem to your conscious mind, your subconscious will continue to pursue it. The more you try to remember, the less likely you will be to recall the information. If you learned the material initially, you will eventually remember it.

Second, create a strategy for remembering. When you can't remember, it's probably because you can't picture the cue that prompts your mind for the actual information. Don't work at trying to remember the information directly. Instead try to remember the cue or manufacture a new cue. For example, if you can't remember somebody's name, begin reciting names in alphabetical order: Abby, Alexandra, Alice, Barbara, Bobbie, Carol, Caroline, Catherine. You may hit on the actual name, but most likely you will recite a name that's similar to the one you're hunting for and the sought-after name will pop into your head. Examine those categories—it is in the categories that you will find "lost" information. Create new groups, as if you were memorizing the information for the first time, and what you want to know will probably come back to you.

About the Author

Bill Adler, Jr., has been teaching memory techniques since 1983. He is the author of six books, including *The Wit and Wisdom of Wall Street, The Lottery Book,* and *The Home Buyer's Guide.* He lives in Washington, D.C. He spends his vacations backpacking in the Maine or Idaho mountains or gathering sun on an undiscovered beach.

TESSA HADLEY is the author of seven highly praised novels, *Accidents in the Home*, which was longlisted for the Guardian First Book Award, *Everything Will Be All Right*, *The Master Bedroom*, *The London Train*, *Clever Girl*, *The Past*, *Late in the Day* and three collections of stories, *Sunstroke*, *Married Love* and *Bad Dreams*.

She won a Windham–Campbell prize for Fiction in 2016, *The Past* won the Hawthornden Prize for 2016, and *Bad Dreams* won the 2018 Edge Hill Short Story Prize. Her stories appear regularly in the *New Yorker*.

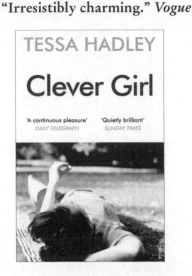

Stella was a clever girl, everyone thought so. Living with her mother and rather unsatisfactory stepfather in suburban respectability she reads voraciously, smokes until her voice is hoarse and dreams of a less ordinary life. When she meets Val, he seems to her to embody everything she longs for — glamour, ideas, excitement and the thrill of the unknown. But these things come at a price and one that Stella despite all her cleverness doesn't realise until it is too late.

"A story that doesn't overreach, about a character who feels real, told in prose that isn't ornate yet is startlingly exact. The effect is a fine and well-chosen pileup of experiences that gather meaning and power." Meg Wolitzer, *New York Times Book Review*

"Tessa Hadley is wonderful at surprising us with the domestic dramas that stir the embers of everyday life." *Toronto Star*

"Like Munro, Hadley is a writer both exact and lyrical, and there are many pleasures to be found along the way, particularly her sensual descriptions of nature, adolescence, and maternity." *The Guardian*

"Few writers give me such consistent pleasure."
Zadie Smith

'Exquisite'   'Brilliant'   'Remarkable'
GUARDIAN   MAIL ON SUNDAY   TATLER

TESSA HADLEY
Bad Dreams

'One of Britain's finest writers'
THE TIMES

The dazzling collection of stories from
the *Sunday Times* bestselling author of *Late in the Day*.

Two sisters quarrel over an inheritance and a new baby. A housekeeper caring for a helpless old man uncovers secrets from his past. A young girl accepts a lift in a car with a group of strangers. An old friend brings bad news to a dinner party.

In these gripping and unsettling stories, the ordinary is made extraordinary and the real things that happen to people turn out to be every bit as mysterious as their dreams.

"These well-turned, exceptionally nuanced pieces are solidly evocative of place, period . . . and sensory detail." *Sunday Times*

"Unflinching, intelligent and fascinating." Marian Keyes

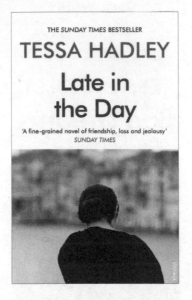

The lives of two close-knit couples are
irrevocably changed by an untimely death in this
Sunday Times bestselling novel.

Alex and Christine and Zach and Lydia have been inseparable since their twenties. From student house-shares and grubby pubs to proper homes and grown-up careers, the two couples' lives have been interlinked for decades. Then one evening, Alex and Christine receive a call from a distraught Lydia. Zach is dead.

Inconsolable, Lydia moves in with Alex and Christine. But instead of their loss bringing them closer, the three of them find that love and sorrow give way to anger and bitterness as old entanglements and resentments rise from the past.

"A fine-grained novel of friendship, loss and jealousy." *Sunday Times*, 100 Great 21st-Century Novels

"Hadley brings the gifts of a still-life painter to her fiction yet manages to produce satisfying twists and turns to her storytelling." *New Statesman*